STUDIES IN APPLIED ANTHROPOLOGY

The Monographs on Social Anthropology were
established in 1940 and aim to publish results of
modern anthropological research of primary interest
to specialists.

The continuation of the series in letterpress has
been made possible by a generous grant-in-aid from
the Wenner-Gren Foundation for Anthropological
Research. Any profits from the series will be returned
to a rotating fund to assist further publication.

The Monographs are under the direction of an
Editorial Board associated with the Department of
Anthropology of the London School of Economics
and Political Science.

LONDON SCHOOL OF ECONOMICS
MONOGRAPHS ON SOCIAL ANTHROPOLOGY
No. 16

Studies
in Applied
Anthropology

by

L. P. MAIR

UNIVERSITY OF LONDON
THE ATHLONE PRESS
1961

First published 1957 *by*
THE ATHLONE PRESS
UNIVERSITY OF LONDON
at 2 *Gower Street, London* WC1
Distributed by Constable & Co. Ltd
12 *Orange Street, London* WC2

Canada
University of Toronto Press

© *L. P. Mair,* 1957

Reprinted 1961

First Printed in Great Britain by
JARROLD AND SONS LTD NORWICH

Reprinted by offset-lithography by
BRADFORD AND DICKENS
Drayton House, London WC1

CONTENTS

FOREWORD

Social anthropology is the study of the systems of co-operation, based on the general recognition of rights and obligations and of the role that each individual is expected to play in the various situations likely to confront him, by which men succeed in living together in some sort of order and harmony. It pursues its inquiries by observation of small groups of people in direct 'face-to-face' relations. Its first field was that of the societies which have variously been called 'primitive', 'simple', 'small-scale', 'peasant', 'pre-literate' and 'pre-industrial'. It may be argued that there are no such societies left; industry with its mass organisation and literacy with its mass media of communication have penetrated everywhere. If this is so, to what and how can our knowledge be applicable?

The answer to the first question is that some of us have directed our attention particularly to the way in which peasant societies have reacted to the impact of 'western' mechanical, scientific civilisation. We see there in an exaggerated form the conflict between the forces making for adherence to tradition and the invitation to depart from it presented by new situations that is characteristic of any society.

At the present time there is a very wide-spread interest in the future of the non-European peoples. The adjective most commonly applied to them is 'under-developed', with its implication that they have to make up lee-way. Where they have recently attained independence, or expect soon to attain it, their leaders are determined to make them into modern states, utilising their resources to the full to provide standards of living and social services comparable with those of older nations. They have the moral backing of many men of good will, and a certain amount of financial backing and expert assistance from the United Nations and groups of states like those that sponsored the Colombo Plan. They do not ask anthropologists to tell them how to achieve their end, and not many of us would offer to do so.

We do claim, however, a certain insight into the processes involved that derives directly from our observations and the theories based on them. This is of practical significance where plans for the betterment of the more 'backward' elements meet with difficulties. The layman is tempted to explain these in psychological terms—'peasant conservatism' and the like. The anthropologist looks to the situation in which the object of the betterment scheme finds himself. What is the strength of the social pressures working on him to conform to tradition? What advantages, social or material, in his accustomed way of life is he being asked to forgo? What does he expect of life, anyway? Can the new schemes be shown to offer him something he values? Sometimes the anthropologist can do a simple job of interpretation to people who

7

just do not know what the life of the people whom they are seeking to improve is like.

Some of these essays were written at a time when the 'backward' peoples had not the voice in the management of their own affairs that they have today, and with colonial policy in British African territories particularly in mind. The dominant theory of those days was that it was better to build on existing institutions than to break violently with the past. Today the view that commands general acceptance is that there is too little time for this; the pace of modernisation must be the fastest possible. This change illustrates my contention that it is not much use to ask an anthropologist what the direction of a colonial policy, or a development policy, ought to be; that will be decided by the pressure of interests outside the scientific field. But the essays in question illustrate my further contention that an anthropologist can 'apply' his special knowledge by making intelligible to the layman the forces at work in the society that he is seeking to change. The facts that were relevant, for example, for a colonial government seeking to preserve traditional authorities are just as relevant for independent governments seeking to supersede them.

Acknowledgments for permission to reprint are due to the Editors of the following journals: *African Affairs (Journal of the African Society), Africa, Oversea Education, World Affairs, Indonesië*, and the *British Journal of Sociology*; and to the Institut Solvay, Brussels, for permission to reproduce a paper given at a conference on Native Economy in Africa.

L. P. M.

I

APPLIED ANTHROPOLOGY AND DEVELOPMENT POLICIES

In the last twenty or thirty years, gallons of ink have been spilt in discussion of the appropriate, or the inevitable, relation between scientific research and social needs, or, in more old-fashioned terms, between 'pure' and 'applied' science. At one extreme, 'pure' science is conceived as the disinterested pursuit of knowledge for its own sake. At the other, Marxist theory asserts that advances in scientific theory occur only in response to the demand for solutions to practical problems, though this does not exclude the value of 'fundamental' research, the bearing of which on practical problems is not immediately obvious to the layman. In the field which this discussion generally covers there is no doubt as to what is meant by applied science. It is the application of principles experimentally established to the production of specific results. In many cases the techniques based on these principles are so well developed that they can be practised by people with no more than an elementary understanding of the principles themselves, and indeed some of them are practised by all of us in everyday life. In others a scientist may be asked to solve a problem which falls in his field, but yet cannot be dealt with by the application of any principle already established; in these cases the functions of the pure and the applied scientist are combined.

Though I have implied by my choice of a title for this book that one can speak in an analogous way of the application of the principles of social anthropology, it must be admitted that the analogy is not a very close one. Indeed, in many quarters it is questioned whether anthropology is a science at all, and among anthropologists themselves there are some who hold that it is not and should not be. It is not, of course, an experimental science; it shares this disability with the other social sciences, apart from psychology, which can be studied experimentally to a limited extent. It can, however, claim to be something more than that study of the unique product of a particular series of events which Evans-Pritchard appears to have had in mind when he described anthropology as essentially akin to history. It does look for regularities in social behaviour extending beyond the limits of a single society, even if these must be of the 'natural history' type and not of the kind that the physicist can express in an equation. It has investigated the validity of theories of 'primitive communism', 'primitive pacifism' and a specifically 'primitive' type of mentality, and has rejected them in favour of interpretations which ascribe the special characteristics of the simpler societies, not to peculiarities in the nature of the people who compose them, but to the limitations of the techniques and resources at their disposal. This is a general proposition verified by observation, though in the nature of the case

9

not by experiment, and it is of the first importance to anyone whose interest in the organisation of these societies arises from a desire to change it. It is the first step away from the assumption that any resistance to changes which the wise Westerner sees as desirable can be due only to laziness, stupidity, superstition or some other defect of character. The next, and indeed the heart of the matter, is the explanation of the complex of social pressures, of recognised claims and obligations, of values inculcated from childhood, within which every individual reacts to the attempts of strangers to improve his character, his way of life or his standard of living.

What anthropologists write when they are trying to interpret the African (as I shall call him for brevity, since I draw my own examples from Africa) to the 'practical man' is quite different from the kind of thing they write when they are analysing and comparing societies for the benefit of other anthropologists. But in the former case, are they acting like applied scientists, or even like the authors of text-books on applied science?

In one very important respect, they are not. Their books are not 'how to do it' manuals, providing formulae for the manipulation of society as the text-books of applied science do for the manipulation of matter. This is not to be explained simply by the relatively undeveloped state of anthropological theory. Indeed, an important achievement of anthropological analysis has been to show how much less easy it is to reshape society by deliberate action than has sometimes been supposed. The phrase 'social engineering', which some of us used with confidence a generation ago, is now out of favour.

The difference in the nature of the contribution that we can make towards the solution of practical problems is inherent in the nature of our subject-matter. That of the natural scientist is inert or without volition; in Africa he is asked to show how the swollen-shoot virus can be controlled, to find a profitable cash crop for an area of poor soils, or a reasonably cheap fertiliser, a prophylactic against malaria or a source of energy in a region with no coal. Attached to his solution is a large proviso which he is allowed to take for granted; his prescription will work *provided that people will use it*. Where it directly affects the mode of life of individuals, the people in question are the public in general; where it involves large-scale activities like the supply of power or irrigation, they are the controllers of the public purse. *As a scientist* he can work out the answer and say, 'Take it or leave it'; though if he happens to be by nature a politician, he will try to present it in palatable form. It is not, however, his professional research that tells him what is or is not palatable; his views on this subject will be drawn from incursions as an amateur into the social field. If, however, he fails to persuade, he has not failed in his task as a scientist; and he always has to face the possibility that a government may decide that what he recommends is too costly for the available resources.

The anthropologist's field of study is society. He cannot deal with a smaller unit than a number of persons linked by a network of socially recognised relationships, and his subject-matter is, not even the persons as organisms, but the completely immaterial relations—of claim and obligation, right and duty, superiority and subordination—that exist between them. If these can be manipulated, and some anthropologists do use the word, it must be in a very different sense from that in which iron ore is treated to make a steel girder or even malaria parasites killed in a human body.

They can, of course, be changed by external influences—directly by penalising customary actions and imposing new obligations, indirectly by offering new opportunities. The civilising mission of Europeans in the tropics, as it used to be called, the diffusion of technical assistance to underdeveloped areas, as it is called today, consists precisely in these processes. In the early period, the emphasis was on the whole more moral, in the latter it is more technological; though, at any rate in those territories for which the United Kingdom is responsible, we are as much interested today in making people democratic as our grandfathers were in making them Christian.

Some of the anthropologists who have given special attention to the social changes that these influences produce describe their work by the adjective 'applied'. The word recalls the confident 'social engineering' days in which it was born, and the fact that, historically, the founders of the International African Institute, the first body to sponsor studies of social change in Africa, expected the research which it promoted to bear fruit in enlightened policies. Predisposed to a sympathetic interpretation of African institutions and to those policies which sought to build on and develop these institutions rather than abruptly substitute others of European type, they expected that intensive field studies would provide governments with the data they were already looking for. To a large extent, they did so. They greatly increased the range of knowledge about the structure and operations of African political systems and about the nature of African civil law, notably in relation to land rights and marriage.

To administrators, however, the operative words have always been 'build' and 'develop', and it is here that the role of anthropologists becomes more difficult. Trained as they are to approach human institutions in an analytical spirit and to recognise how much all moral judgments are culturally conditioned, they do not necessarily share the administrators' assumptions as to what constitutes progress. On the other hand, they do not follow Westermarck's theory of ethical relativity to its logical conclusion of complete neutrality between different policies. When they have argued that the improvements which administrators have sought to make in the institutions of subject peoples were in fact no improvement, they have not taken their stand on the ground that there would be nothing to choose between the first state and the last, but have defended traditional institutions in terms of values shared by themselves and the administrators. Some have held the view that the colonial status is wrong in itself, and have argued that to integrate tribal political authorities in a colonial administrative system is a way of perpetuating this status and so deserves no assistance from them.[1] Some have combined both attitudes. The second has something in common with that of the extreme pacifist who will not even succour the victims in a war. Granted that colonial policy has always taken into account, and often unduly, the interests of the imperial Power and its nationals, there is some room in every dependent territory, and a good deal in some, for action genuinely intended to further the interests of the inhabitants, and it is in this sphere that knowledge of their social organisation is relevant. Some anthropologists, however, serve governments like that of the Union of South Africa, whose policies other anthropologists deplore; and this has been quoted as an instance of the use of scientific knowledge for anti-social ends.[2]

In the politically dependent territories, the refusal of anthropologists to buttress colonial rule has in fact had little part in its decline, and already the government of many of the tropical countries has passed to people who are alien only by culture and not by birth from the mass of their population. Of more significance have been the consequences of the development of anthropological studies themselves on the one hand and of policy on the other. The farther studies of African political institutions were pursued, the clearer it became that the 'Native Administrations' recognised by colonial governments had nothing but their personnel in common with their traditional predecessors; and in the sphere of civil law, though many people still sought to uphold traditional usage, as many were finding it to their interest to adopt the relationships characteristic of the modern commercial economy. The analysis of this process has been a valuable contribution to the study of society in general, but the conclusion to which it leads is that policies based on the preservation of traditional institutions, to which anthropological data were directly relevant, are now no longer practicable. Yet another conclusion which we cannot escape is that rapid technological change imposes a severe strain on small-scale societies. Its first result is a breakdown of traditional sanctions, and these are not easily replaced. Some American anthropologists go so far as to say that it produces a 'disturbance of basic personality'.

The older philosophy that was epitomised in the phrase 'Indirect Rule' has in fact been rejected. But in this development too anthropologists have had little part. It has been brought about mainly by the emergence of a western-educated class of political leaders in the dependent territories, who are committed to radical changes in both political and economic spheres, in a climate of world opinion sympathetic to their aspirations. Auxiliary influences have been that of the Western Powers, who, fearing that poverty may drive the tropical peoples to Communism, have a new motive for wishing to see their

[1] Cf. R. W. Firth, *Human Types*, 1938, pp. 195-7.
[2] S. F. Nadel, *Anthropology and Modern Life*, 1953, p. 9.

standards of living rise; of a considerable number of individuals who desire the same thing on purely humanitarian grounds; and of some technical authorities who have drawn attention to the dangerous destruction of natural resources by the farming methods of the tropical peasant. Faced with this last argument, the anthropologist cannot easily dismiss as 'materialistic' policies which must destroy the old social bonds; and indeed most of us, at times when the role of amateur doctor was forced upon us in the field, must have reflected that such medical services as are provided in the dependent territories are financed out of those very developments whose social consequences we have been deploring, and have felt that a good deal of social disturbance might be worth while if it raised the wretchedly low standard of health.

If it did. It is one thing to say that health cannot be improved without development, quite another that development is bound to improve health. The new rulers who believed that colonial exploitation was responsible for all their ills, the technical assistance teams who are offering their 'know-how' to the 'under-developed areas', are facing a problem that neither freedom nor technology can solve—how to induce the peasantry, in Furnivall's memorable phrase, to 'want what they need'.

Sometimes they turn to the anthropologist for the answer, particularly in America, where this kind of problem is new, and anthropologists have not yet lost the confidence that some of us in Britain once had. Why should not the anthropologist's 'how-to-do-it' manual complement those of the health visitor and agricultural extension worker? This brings us back to our starting-point—the content of the word 'it'.

The medical and the agricultural expert base their advice on 'prediction' in the simple sense that, in the field where their theories have been experimentally verified, they can say that what has happened before will happen again; certain biochemical processes will have certain consequences. Anthropologists—some of whom experience much heart-searching and sense of inferiority about the inability of their science to 'predict'—are being asked, in this context, not only to manipulate the immaterial, but to deal with situations the essence of which is that, in the anthropologists' field of inquiry, *they have not happened before.* In so far as the demand comes from outside and is not provoked by the anthropologists themselves, those who make it are either impelled by the naive belief that there must be a technique for every problem, or think of 'natives' as having a specific 'mentality' the 'reactions' of which ought to be forseeable by people who 'study natives'.

But the anthropologist's central problem is the nature of the forces that keep a society in being, that secure respect for accepted standards and some approximation to them of actual behaviour—in a word, the forces of conservatism. In so far as we can see regularities in human society, it is in the field of behaviour which is in accordance with these standards, and in the type of sanctions which secure

13

uniformity. They are our nearest analogue, however distant, to the properties of material substances. Anthropologists who take a special interest in social change—and not all anthropologists do, for many think the study of established systems should be their primary task—inquire what are the circumstances in which new influences will be stronger than those making for conformity. But they too are aware that the mixture of rational calculations of advantage and culturally conditioned assumptions which maintains any social structure in being cannot be synthesised. It would be meaningless to ask an anthropologist to invent a new institution; it is the nature of the phenomena, not the inadequacy of his science, that makes this so. What he can do is to show where and why resistance is likely to be shown to innovations the merits of which may seem to their sponsors to be self-evident. This is not so insignificant an achievement that he need be ashamed of it. It is also sometimes possible for him, generalising from the experience of other societies than the one under consideration, to foresee the implications of a proposed policy over a wider field than that which it directly envisages; this is 'prediction', as far as it goes.

The nearest approach to a 'how-to-do-it' manual comes from America, where E. H. Spicer[3] has collected a number of instances where social factors blocked the introduction of technical improvements, presenting 'problem' and 'answer' separately so that students can try to work out their own solution. The solutions given consist for the most part in advice either on what to avoid or on what kinds of resistance to expect; a new cereal may give a better yield but not make such good pancakes, and some other innovation may involve too difficult a re-organisation of the labour force, a protest movement among mining labourers may have a social background very different from that which engendered the C.I.O. These are aids to analysis of the situation, and valuable aids; they are not prescriptions for action. The nearest approach to such a prescription is the advice to look for the group within which the sense of solidarity is strong enough to predispose its members to co-operate in new activities which can be shown to be in their interests.

R. W. Firth is the leading exponent in Britain of the view that the anthropologist's knowledge can be best utilised not in prescribing policies but in calling attention to the possibly unforeseen implications of the policies proposed by governments. To him this follows from the fact that the major premises of policy are predetermined, and that though the anthropologist may deny their validity he is not free to disregard them. I have suggested that it is in fact an inescapable result of the nature of our study; I shall have something to say later about the evaluation of policy by anthropologists. Firth illustrates his own principle in an excellent article[4] on the social implications of

---

[3] *Human Problems in Technological Change*, 1952.
[4] 'Some Social Aspects of the Colombo Plan', *Westminster Bank Review*, May 1951, pp. 1–7.

14

the Colombo Plan. In this he calls attention to the consequences of creating a middle class of technicians wholly dependent on their profession, if the speed of development is allowed to slacken so that many of these find themselves without employment. How to prevent this is clearly not a problem for an anthropologist; yet it takes a student of society to look beyond the simple assumption that 'development' will cure 'poverty' and so allay discontent, and foresee this situation. He also indicates the very radical change in the peasant's mode of life, and in the social relationships dependent on land rights, that are involved in proposals to substitute swamp cultivation for hill cultivation of rice; and insists that the advantages of such a change will have to be presented in very cogent form if they are to be accepted. Finally he explains some of the social attitudes that militate against that disposition to save and invest which, according to economists, is so necessary if people are to achieve the increase in productivity which will eventually raise their standard of living. Firth has also followed his own counsel that the anthropologist's function is to indicate the implications of alternative policies, and leave governments to choose between them, in a discussion of possible remedies for over-population in Tikopia.[5] Other examples of advice given in this form are rare.

These arguments are based on the results of general study of the peoples concerned, not on special inquiries made with the aim of 'applying'—that is, somehow ultilising—the data obtained. The term 'applied anthropology' has sometimes been used also of investigations in which anthropologists have collaborated with other specialists in fields where the latter hope to take action. Several such studies have been made on the subject of nutrition; in these dieticians have investigated the adequacy of the food consumed by some selected community while agricultural experts have studied techniques of cultivation and anthropologists the aspects of social organisation relevant to the production, preparation and consumption of food. A study of a rather different type[6] was recently made by M. Freedman in Indonesia, where, in connection with a WHO campaign against kwashi-orkor, he looked for social factors with which the prevalence of the disease might be correlated and at the same time for explanations of the effectiveness or otherwise of nutrition propaganda. His specific recommendations are concerned with the organisation and training of health workers; again, more 'What should they *know*?' than 'What should they *do*?' His own researches cover local attitudes towards food, health and medical practice; the validity of assumptions made in our own culture about the social factors leading to illness in children and of assumptions made by Indonesian doctors about the ideas and practices of their own patients; the type of propaganda which is understood; circumstances such as the organisation of household work

[5] *We, The Tikopia*, 1936, Chap. XII.
[6] Unpublished.

15

or the low level of family income which may make it impracticable for people to follow the health educator's advice. In sum, it is a most valuable statement of the circumstances in which public health campaigns must operate. It also makes the point, which not only anthropologists have made before, that a campaign has little hope of success unless it enlists the support of influential persons in the community, and it gives the kind of information that anthropologists are best qualified to give as to where such persons are likely to be found. This again is not a 'how-to-do-it' manual but rather a map of territory previously unexplored.

A valiant attempt to produce a theoretical principle which would be generally applicable in practice has been made by C. S. Belshaw. He indeed seems to imply adherence to the view that no theoretical generalisation which is not a guide to action has 'justification'.[7] Writing with reference to development policies in colonial territories he argues that they consist essentially in altering 'the preference structure of a community'. But his actual prescriptions are not guides to action. One is that the balance of advantages of any policy against its cost should be calculated in terms of the values of the society concerned—a general principle, that of toleration or consideration of local wishes, which is not new, though it is seldom formulated in the language of the economist. The other is that 'ends', as he likes to call the aims of policy, to be accepted must be understood, and must not involve a conflict with social pressures inherent in the society which are too strong to be resisted. Since he believes that our science, now in its infancy, will advance to a much higher degree of precision in the future, he may hope that we shall one day produce formulae for detecting and measuring social pressures. But he does not even suggest any formula for directing them. So we again find that in practice the function of the anthropologist is to point to resistances inherent in social relationships, and also, of course, to 'growing points'. Why should he claim more? We are not specialists in public relations or in the art of persuasion.

S. F. Nadel also claims an important place for the anthropologist in practical affairs, and would sometimes seem to suggest, as Malinowski did, that the comprehensive scope of anthropology as the study of society as a whole should give his views priority over those of technical specialists in other fields. His own writings include examples of inquiries made at the request of governments, recommendations to governments, and forecasts of the consequences of existing trends arising from studies made without any practical aim. He has also asserted in general terms that, however inadequate the anthropologist's theories in comparison with those of the natural scientist, they nevertheless take him a good deal farther than the layman, and that if his advice is sought the blunders that he makes will at least be 'better blunders'.[8]

[7] *Changing Melanesia*, 1954, p. 156.
[8] *Foundations of Social Anthropology*, 1951, p. 55.

When we examine the points on which Nadel has made practical recommendations, however, we find that for the most part they belong to fields in which those in authority wish to recognise existing institutions and the main question asked is simply what these are. His study of the Nuba tribes of Kordofan was undertaken to provide the Sudan government with general information on their political system and civil law; it has some interesting remarks on the prerequisites for a successful federation for local government purposes.[9] When with the occupation forces in Eritrea he recorded the customary system of land rights;[10] and in writing of the Nupe of the Northern Region of Nigeria he made an interesting estimate of the probable consequences of the introduction of mixed farming.[11] From a personal communication I learn that on one occasion during the war he successfully opposed the imposition of collective punishment on certain Somali tribes on the ground that this was not in fact consistent with their customs and would not hit the persons at whom it was aimed. Each of these examples made a valuable addition to the information in the possession of a government. None of them, however, enters that contemporary field of policies aiming at extensive change which cannot be ignored if claims are made by anthropologists, or demands made on them, without reservation.

In opposition to the view I have suggested, that we deal with a subject-matter which is by its nature not susceptible of manipulation, both Belshaw and Nadel use the word, the former of something he thinks desirable, the latter of something that he considers dangerous. Belshaw appears to have in mind the secondary meaning of the word, that of 'using to one's advantage', since he describes policies in general as 'attempts to manipulate social processes'. Nadel, when he says the anthropologist can 'suggest how societies can be manipulated', implies something very sinister if this use of the word is intended. Possibly both writers are approaching the same subject from different points of view. Though it is unlikely that many men of affairs have much idea of what is meant by a social process, it is probable that, if they did, they might see more clearly the possibilities and limitations of political action and so frame their policies more intelligently; and this would be an element in that appreciation of the obstacles to be overcome which I have described as the anthropologist's most significant contribution to practical affairs. It is generally assumed that the policies in question are well-intentioned; and it is agreed that, if an anthropologist had reason to doubt this in a given case, he would be justified in refusing his co-operation. Nadel, however, considers that the 'manipulation of a society' might be for ends harmful to it, and that even if he refused to offer practical advice, an anthropologist might contribute to this simply by publishing facts. It is clear that this is a

[9] *The Nuba,* 1947, pp. 492–3.
[10] 'Land Tenure on the Eritrean Plateau', *Africa,* vol. xvi, pp. 1–22, 99–109.
[11] *A Black Byzantium,* 1942, pp. 367–8.

logical possibility; but before regarding it as a serious potential danger one would like to hear some examples of such hypothetical situations. It is in this context that Nadel quotes the Union of South Africa. He asks if the knowledge of anthropology is 'employed to buttress the obtaining policy and to strengthen the subjection of the native peoples'.[12] To answer this question one would need to know not only more about the kind of information that is in fact collected by the ethnologists of the Department of Native Affairs, but also what kind of application is envisaged. Ethnographic data could perhaps be quoted to confirm the Nationalist view that Africans, as 'primitive' people, differ in something essential from Europeans; the burden of proving that they could be used in any other way to further the illiberal aspects of the *apartheid* policy, or to frustrate movements of opposition to it, would seem to lie with the maker of the suggestion. Nadel also refers to the use made by the United States government, in the late war, of anthropological studies of the 'character structure' of their enemies in planning 'psychological warfare'. Only an expert in this branch of anthropology could express a view on its effectiveness as a weapon of destruction.

Nevertheless, one cannot discuss the bearing of any branch of knowledge on practice without considering the responsibility of the scientist. Is this limited to increasing knowledge? Is it his right, or his duty, to demand a say in the activities for which his knowledge is used? Not many scientific discoveries have been as obviously double-edged as that of nuclear fission, which has so catastrophically become the *locus classicus* for this discussion. If the neutrality of anthropologists is not really likely to result in a disaster to humanity or even to the peoples among whom they have worked, it may yet be that they do not wish to remain neutral, but would like to be regarded as specially qualified to say what colonial, or other, social policies ought to be. Also, they may be told that if they stop short of this they are not giving the full benefit of their knowledge to the world.

The social sciences occupy a different position from the natural sciences in this discussion, because ethical judgments are not external to their field of research but at the very centre of it. When social scientists present their results, they are describing human actions, on which their readers will pass judgment even if they themselves do not explicitly do so; and the way in which their description is worded will influence that judgment. The 'functional theory' in its extreme form held that the institutions of every society solved the problems of mastery of the environment through social co-operation in the way best suited to that society. Such a theory precludes any attempt to rank different societies in order of merit, but in order to make it convincing its adherents have to take every opportunity of defending institutions popularly regarded as 'barbarous' to a public that will not accept a defence based on the principle of toleration alone. Hence they are at once involved in appeals to the ethical assumptions of their

[12] *Anthropology and Modern Life*, p. 9.

18

public. Another theory is that, since all values are culturally determined, it is only our cultural conditioning that leads us to disapprove of any feature of an alien culture. Looked at without this subjective bias, all institutions are equally worthy of respect (or at least should be criticised only by people living under them). This theory has various weaknesses; it is inconsistent in that it makes a *Herrenvolk* attitude, which is a denial of itself, equally valid with one of 'cross-cultural' tolerance, and it has been pointed out that respect for alien cultures is itself an ethical principle.

It is obvious that anthropologists, who, like the rest of humanity, live as members of society, must recognise ethical principles in relation to their own actions, and it is unlikely that they will remain completely unmoved when confronted with actions among the peoples they study which run counter to the principles they cherish most.[13] Some have felt it a moral imperative to intervene to prevent homicide; such a necessity, fortunately, is rare. We have to try to practise a kind of emotional anaesthesia in the presence of values which may shock us, and to represent them as fairly as possible in our writings. In fact, however, most anthropologists have gone farther. Most of us have come to regard the peoples we have lived among as our friends, and have wished to give a sympathetic interpretation of them to readers who may include impatient emissaries of material, and indignant emissaries of moral, uplift. Our experience of people who follow different standards from our own need not lead us to the conclusion that there is nothing to choose between different types of society, but it may lead us to a profitable examination of the question how far the rules of our own are rationally defensible.

If we abandon the principle of ethical neutrality, or, alternatively, find that we have never really held it, does this involve us in any practical consequences? R. Redfield, who in his Messenger Lectures has argued most persuasively against the principle, gives as one reason for rejecting it the fact that it is no use to an anthropologist who is consulted about a Point Four programme[14]—that is, of course, if the anthropologist is willing to help with the Point Four programme. This argument once more brings in what I suggest is the fallacy of supposing that the role of the anthropologist in the execution of these programmes ought to be a directing one. Anthropologists may have a higher status in the United States than they do in Britain, but my guess is that it must only be a matter of time before they learn by experience that their contribution must be limited in the way I have suggested by the nature of our subject. Though it doubtless depends upon individual temperament how much any anthropologist wishes to be employed as a consultant, I do not agree that to confine oneself to indicating the implications of policy is a cowardly shirking of issues, still less a refusal to put one's knowledge at the service of humanity.

[13] This situation is admirably treated in fictional form in E. Smith-Bowen, *Return to Laughter*, 1954.
[14] *The Primitive World and its Transformations*, 1953, p. 145.

The question is sometimes discussed as if anthropologists were offered the opportunity of making recommendations over the whole field of policy, or at least invited to choose between alternatives. I am not aware that this has ever happened, but if it did, I cannot see that we could do otherwise, even if we had a definite preference for one, than make clear the social implications of both; that is, assuming that we are expected, like other advisers, to present a reasoned case. There remains the situation where an anthropologist may consider that some actual or proposed policy calls for a protest made in the light of his knowledge of its effects or implications. Anthropologists have not in fact imposed upon themselves any self-denying ordinance in the matter of protests. But when they protest, they must distinguish between their private moral code and their professional authority. We have no right to claim to be arbiters of morals, though of course we can argue that an actual or proposed policy is contrary to the moral principles to which its promoters subscribe; and, indeed, we need not expect to be listened to if we based a protest on any other grounds.

Though the makers of policy do not invite anthropologists to be their mentors, there are other sections of society where more is expected of us. It can happen that groups of people interested in promoting political principles seek the specialist assistance of social scientists, and ask from them not only information but programmes. They approach the subject, perhaps, with the expectation of the young H. G. Wells that the application of the appropriate sciences can re-make the world; and when the hungry sheep are not fed with what they ask for, they are sometimes displeased and accuse the scientist of failing in his duty to society. But it is pertinent to ask whether the role of sheep is the appropriate one for them in this context. They do not choose their adviser for his sympathy with their aims, assuming, no doubt, that there is one right line which any expert in the subject would give. This is the moment to remember that anthropologists, so far from being ethically neutral, can be found to support quite different programmes. Though I have suggested that alarms about the use that might be made of the *data* supplied by government ethnologists in the Union of South Africa are exaggerated, there is little doubt that, if they were pressed to lay down general principles of *policy*, they would support those of *apartheid*. This might come as a shock to their audience, since in practice there is a certain association of the belief in the scientist as saviour with the belief that there are minimum human rights which the *apartheid* policy denies. But the logic of the position the sheep have taken up should lead them to accept it. Of course the sheep, who are not entirely imaginary, will not do so, but, idealists as they are, will turn on the shepherd as indignantly as they do on the anthropologist who does not undertake to lead them. In fact, at bottom they are not really sheep.

Nor should they be. They, too, like the policy-makers, have really chosen their ends in advance, and it is because it is their right and duty to do so that anthropologists should not claim to take over this decision from them. When Godfrey Wilson wrote that the anthropologist 'cannot, as a scientist, judge of good and evil . . . He can never either approve or condemn any policy as such',[15] he was not putting up a smokescreen to cover retreat but refusing to be guilty of a monstrous arrogance. It is of some interest to note that the second sentence is followed almost immediately by a description of the social consequences of the labour policy of Northern Rhodesia that leaves the reader in no doubt whatever about his opinion of it. The greater the prestige accorded to the scientist, the more essential it is that both he and the public should distinguish what he can from what he cannot claim to *know*. There may be occasions on which, despairing of making his reasoning understood, he falls back on 'I'm not arguing with you. I'm telling you'; but he must not do this in fields where he could not argue from the data of his science. The nature of human welfare and, even more, the sometimes agonising choice between the interests of different groups or between incompatible ends, which are both in themselves desirable, are matters lying within these fields.

The recent discussion in the Press of the British Government's decision to prohibit the manufacture of heroin illustrates some of these points. Most of those who took part in it assumed that the prevention of pain was the end to be chosen, and argued the merits of heroin against other drugs. Some said the wrong experts had been consulted; specialists in medicine, yes, but in the wrong branches. A former League of Nations official, invoking another field of specialist knowledge, pointed out that measures other than forbidding manufacture had been found more effective against the drug traffic in the past. Some argued that any good that could be done in this direction would be outweighed by the suffering of patients who could not be treated with heroin (and would only benefit other nations anyway). Eventually five members of the Standing Medical Advisory Committee wrote a letter re-affirming the medical grounds of their advice, but adding that the choice between the social values in conflict 'cannot be made by doctors alone but only by the Government'.[16] To this the angry rejoinder was made that 'we are told to leave it to Big Brother'.

This very succinct comment suggests, first of all, that the right of a doctor to complete freedom in prescribing treatment must be accepted as having priority over all other considerations; the analogy for an anthropologist might be a demand for priority at all times for a policy calculated to promote social stability, or satisfy national aspirations, or respect native values. It also suggests that, in leaving it to the makers of policy to resolve the conflict, we are treating them as repositories of superior knowledge. In fact we recognise their fallibility to the extent of requiring them to submit to the judgment of the general public at regular intervals, and this is not solely in order to allow groups whose material interests are opposed to compete for the control of policy. It is also because we all have, however dim,

[15] 'Anthropology as a Public Service', *Africa*, 1940, vol. xiii, pp. 45–61.
[16] *Times*, November 30, 1955.

confused, inconsistent, self-interested, prejudiced, some idea of the difference between right and wrong action, and try to select to make the choice for us in cases as they arise people who we believe will decide in accordance with our ideas. Democracy may be easily deceived, as we are constantly reminded nowadays, but the remedy is not to surrender to someone claiming authority the control of that psychological process that old-fashioned people call conscience. We need more people, not fewer, to think about moral questions, and make up their own minds where the right course lies.

I do not suggest that they do this by some sort of innate moral faculty, and I do suggest, as I have said earlier in this essay, that they can be helped by knowledge of the different ways in which mankind has tried to solve the universal problems of living in society. Ginsberg points out that though moral judgments are 'ultimately traceable to primary experiences of value', they do rest on assumptions about facts, and it is for the social scientist to inquire into the validity of these assumptions. He remarks that to establish a rationally based moral system of general validity there is need for more 'inquiry into human needs and the laws of social interaction'.[17] Here there is room for data from the simpler as well as the 'higher societies'.

Nadel suggests that certain criteria of evaluation are, as he puts it, 'entailed' in the concept of 'society' which is basic to social anthropology. 'Integration, regularity, stability, permanence are all requirements of society as we conceive of it: their disappearance means the dissolution of that very entity, society, and their strength or weakness a measure of social existence.' In addition, in the psychological field every culture allows gratifications and imposes frustrations, and the adequacy of any given culture may be assessed in terms of the relationship between the two. These two criteria may, of course, conflict, if, for example, social stability is maintained by 'the rigid exercise of force'; and in judging of such a situation we must, he admits, 'rely on our private convictions'. An anthropologist's training, however, leads him to think 'not only as a citizen or as a human being aware of ethical issues, but as one for whom citizenship and awareness of ethical issues are themselves problems challenging intellectual effort'. Despite all the difficulties which he recognises, he asserts that the anthropologist's judgments on the worthiness of ends are more unassailable than those of others.[18] Those anthropologists who do not subscribe to dogmatic moral systems are certainly entitled to claim that they base such judgments on the rational interpretation of observed data, and those of their fellow-citizens who wish to reach their own conclusions in a rational manner can profit by the study of their arguments. But when the judgment itself is in question, if they ask him to make it for them they must remember that they are crediting him with wisdom as well as knowledge, and that wisdom is not a professional attainment.

[17] *The Diversity of Morals*, 1954, p. 13.
[18] *Anthropology and Modern Life*, p. 16 ff.

II

THE GROWTH OF ECONOMIC INDIVIDUALISM
IN AFRICAN SOCIETY

The title of this paper may give the impression that I intend to reconstruct some process of development from a hypothetical primitive communistic society to one that more nearly approximates to the economic order which we call individualistic. What I do propose is to indicate the nature of the changes which the economic organisation of most native societies has undergone through its contact with Western civilisation. But the process which I shall attempt to describe will, I hope, appear not as a revolutionary transformation from one type of economic organisation to another diametrically opposed to it, still less as an alteration in that alien mentality with which primitive people are so readily endowed by anthropologists and others, but rather as the response to changed circumstances of forces which, in fact, were inherent in these societies, and are not essentially different from what we know among ourselves.

The theory of primitive communism has been found not to square with the facts of any known primitive society. Anthropologists no longer go into the field equipped to discover traces of such an original state. But at the very point where accurate anthropological knowledge is of vital practical importance—in the treatment of those problems of policy which modern conditions have created for colonial administrations—we still find it assumed as axiomatic that there is some fundamental difference between the African attitude to property and our own. Even if the word 'communist' is no longer used, the attempt persists to describe this supposed difference by some such term as 'communalist' or 'collectivist', and the starting-point of discussions of the results of European contact is a brief description of the salient characteristics of a society of this type. One need only refer to such a recent and authoritative study as Major Orde-Browne's analysis of the African labour problem, or to the standard works of M. Delafosse on the cultures of West Africa.

This method of approach confuses the issue in two ways. In the first place, it emphasises apparent differences between African and European economic systems while altogether neglecting points of resemblance. In the second, the attempt to force all African societies into a single category means that undue stress is laid on one or two features which appear to be common to all, while the complete analysis of any one case is neglected. Yet for a real understanding of the effects of European economic contact such an analysis is an essential preliminary. In particular we require a fuller study of those limitations on the disposal of property which are inconsistent with what we call individualism. Such a study, I think, will show that these limitations exist as much because of the limited satisfaction which the

23

possession of property affords in a primitive society as because of the supposed domination of the individual by the group to which he belongs.

I propose to illustrate my argument from the Ganda, the African tribe of which I have personal knowledge, though I think the conclusions would be borne out by data from other peoples not only in Africa but elsewhere.

The Ganda are one of a group of related tribes—the so-called Lacustrian Bantu—who inhabit the northern and western shores of Lake Victoria. All this region was overrun some 300 years ago by an invasion of pastoral Hamitic peoples from the north, who established their domination over the indigenous Bantu agriculturists. In the other kingdoms there is still a cleavage, the extent of which varies from tribe to tribe, between the ruling class and their subjects, but with the Ganda the fusion has been complete. The whole tribe is predominantly agricultural, and there is no hereditary aristocracy. The marks of the conquest are nevertheless apparent in a strongly centralised political organisation which has to a great extent destroyed the importance of the clan as a political and economic, and even as a religious, unit.

In such a society I propose to consider what were the forms of property most highly prized and for what reasons, and how such forms of property were acquired—what constituted a man wealthy and how he became so.

The answer will appear from a description of the political organisation, which will, I hope, demonstrate that the acquisition of wealth was always an object of ambition to the Ganda, so much so that it formed an important incentive to the observance of political obligations and the exercise of certain socially approved qualities.

Among the Ganda the economic and political systems were closely connected through the fact that the administration of land was one of the functions of political authorities. In theory all the land and everything in it belonged to the king. This principle rationalised his economic privileges such as the right to tribute and to a large proportion of the booty captured in war, but did not, of course, mean in fact that he could deal just as he pleased with the property of his subjects. The king appointed chiefs to authority over certain areas of land and their population. Every peasant—to use the most convenient term—had to perform certain services for the chief to whose district he belonged and to turn out at his orders for war or for work required by the king, such as building in the capital or weeding paths. He was liable to be expelled, not only for failure to fulfil these obligations, but also for committing a crime or for displeasing the chief in any way. But if his general behaviour was satisfactory, his occupation in the piece of land first allotted to him remained undisturbed, unless he himself wished to leave it, when it reverted to the disposal of the chief. He could pass it on to his heirs, and successive occupation for two or three generations created a prescriptive right which it was difficult for the chief to overrule.

This system, I might remark in passing, gives considerable rights to the individual, even if they fall short of those comprised in freehold tenure. Its effect was, however, that land could not be utilised as a source of economic advantage in any other way than by cultivation. The status of a wealthy man could not be attained by the exercise of rights over land as such—by bargaining the use of surplus land against some other commodity in any form of sale or lease. This is a very important difference between the traditional and the modern system.

What, then, did make the difference between rich and poor among the Ganda—a difference which was always a clearly marked feature of their system? To an extent much greater than is the case with us the difference was simply one of quantity. With us any household living above subsistence level turns an increase of income, not to the acquisition of more goods exactly like those which it already has, but to the purchase of a better quality, or of other goods which previously were out of its reach. But in conditions which did not offer the innumerable alternatives to which we are accustomed, the mere difference of less and more was much more important. The rich man had abundance of foodstuffs and a store of barkcloths for clothes and bedding. This was a matter much less of individual hard work or thrift, for there is practically no storing of food in this tribe, than of the size of the household. That again depended upon the number of wives, and, still more, on the number of slaves—while to have slaves to do the harder tasks which otherwise fell to the women of the household was in itself a mark of social superiority. Moreover, in a large household some of the wives would be slave-women married without the payment of any bride-price. Over and above this abundance of everyday necessities, the rich man was distinguished by the possession of cattle. While a poor man who owned a cow is not altogether inconceivable, it is always assumed that cattle were the prerogative and hall-mark of the wealthy.

Now, none of these goods were acquired primarily by means of exchange. Of course the everyday commodities, which anyone could make, were not. Slaves may have been bought, though I doubt it. Cattle sometimes were. But it was not by a patient process of adding one to one, of bartering the proceeds of his own or his wife's labours, that the Ganda attained to their possession in numbers sufficient to constitute him a rich man. The way in which this ambition was achieved was always, ultimately, by conduct pleasing to his political superior, and, immediately, by attaining to a position of political authority carrying with it economic privilege.

Thus the main method of increasing the stocks of cattle was by raiding neighbouring tribes, particularly the Banyoro in the northwest. By these raids, too, slaves were acquired. The whole country was organised for such a foray on the command of the king, and theoretically all the spoil belonged to him. What actually happened was that it was first collected at the capital, each chief bringing in the cattle and prisoners taken by his own followers. The king selected his share and the rest was left to the chiefs, who in turn kept a proportion of each man's booty for themselves and left the remainder to the actual captors. The common man's share was roughly proportionate to his own efforts, but how much of his own spoil he was allowed to keep depended a good deal on the terms on which he stood with his chief. As for the chief, what he got out of a foray depended partly on his own and his followers' courage, but also on their mere numbers. The more of them there were, the greater the quantity of cattle and slaves on which he could levy toll. And their numbers were a matter partly of his own popularity, since a peasant might attach himself to any chief, partly of his favour with the king, who could set him over a populous or a small village at his pleasure.

The privileges which the chiefs exercised in this respect extended also to another commodity—the barkcloths from which clothing, bedding, and hangings were made. It was in this commodity that taxes were paid; that is to say, from time to time a levy was organised by the king, who sent his messengers all through the country. Each man had to contribute two barkcloths, which after a fairly late date they were allowed to commute for cowry-shells. Every chief was responsible for the contribution of his own peasants, and was allowed —under the supervision of the royal messenger—to remove his share from the total before the bundles were sent off to the capital. A chief also took his share of the goods paid over in compensation for any offence which was tried in his court.

Thus it was mainly through exercising a chief's privileges that a Ganda became rich. We must next consider how he could attain to such a privileged position. It should be emphasised that this was a matter of individual ability, for political authority was not a matter of hereditary status, but of appointment and promotion by the king. To become a chief was every peasant's ambition. A boy might have the initial advantage of being related to some great chief who could recommend him to the king, but the degree of his advancement was mainly a question of his own merit, and every son of a chief could not count on becoming a chief. Any peasant, even though he had not such a lucky start, if his chief was pleased with him, might be presented to the king with a view to his being appointed a chief.

What, then, were the qualities which a Ganda must display if he wished to become wealthy? Clearly not those which we are accustomed to associate with economic activity—industry, thrift, foresight, skill in bargaining. Trade did exist, as a means of obtaining certain objects when required, but nobody engaged in it continuously in order to increase the total of his possessions. To this goal a chief's position was the only road. To reach such a position, then, a man had to behave in a manner approved by his superiors; to prosper in it the approval of his inferiors was also necessary.

A peasant earned the favour of his chief by such qualities as obedience, loyalty, flattery if you like; by making presents over and above the services which were a matter of legal obligation; above all by constant attendance at the chief's council. If the chief was an important man with many followers, this attendance was essential to make the chief aware of his existence. The two fields in which he could earn signal merit were those of council and of war. Both courage in battle and wisdom in council were rewarded by the chief, and both were qualities which led to a man's appointment as a chief and subsequent promotion.

The king expected of his chiefs very much the same behaviour as a chief did of his peasants. But a chief had also to prove himself worthy of his position by retaining the loyalty of his followers. It has been mentioned that a peasant was free to move from one chief to another at any time, and the merits of a chief were gauged very largely by his popularity as indicated by the number of his peasants. A chief whose following was noticeably on the decline would be moved by the king to a smaller village. Apart from this, it was clearly to his advantage, in view of the privileges which we have described, to have as many peasants under his authority as he could.

A peasant expected his chief to be just, affable, and liberal in making feasts for his people when they had finished a piece of work for him and possibly at other times, in helping the unfortunate, perhaps by the payment of a debt or fine, and in generously rewarding merit. So much was this liberality expected of a chief that I have heard a native defend his privileges on the ground that without them 'he could not make his people rich'. The man who was rich on a smaller scale—a fortunate peasant, for instance—was similarly expected to excel his neighbours in hospitality and in the scale on which he made gifts on those occasions when ritual required it, and to help his relatives in difficulties.

So we seem to have returned to the communistic savage, who acquires wealth only to give it away. But is this the whole of the story? Does the value set on generous giving really mean that the giver is not interested in acquiring and possessing the goods that he distributes? Surely the whole system that I have described, with its emphasis on the rewards in kind that virtue can earn, its distinction between the standards of lavishness of rich and poor, proves the very contrary.

What, then, are the essential differences between this system and our own? They seem to be two in number. In the first place, in a society of such relatively simple structure the position of a chief was practically the only one to which social prestige was attached. An exception must be made for the practitioner of magic, who could become both wealthy and powerful, but this career was only open to people with special psychological characteristics. Otherwise the brave man, the wise judge, the cunning flatterer, alike had only this one way of making their mark. Talent and ambition had not to choose, as they have with us, between a career whose rewards are mainly material and one less lucrative but carrying with it, perhaps, a more

27

desirable social status or a particularly attractive kind of power. The different types of social prestige which appeal to different temperaments were combined in one position. No one can say what motive weighed strongest with any one of the old-time Ganda who set himself to rise in life; but it is certain that this was a matter of individual ambition, and that in many cases the wealth attached to authority was a reason for desiring it.

Looked at from another angle, the significant difference is that there was no purely economic means of acquiring wealth. It could not be amassed through a series of impersonal transactions to which the moral qualities of the parties were irrelevant; its acquisition depended very largely on the supposed possession of characteristics which met with general social approval. It depended also, of course, on the arbitrary favour of superior persons, whose judgment of character was by no means unbiassed or infallible. But it was not a matter of economic competition between individuals, or, indeed, of competition, in the sense of rivalry in the pursuit of a limited reward, at all. To that extent, in the traditional system, ambition was perhaps directed along channels less socially disruptive than those which it follows in the same society today.

The other difference lies in the kind of satisfaction which superior wealth gives to its possessor. The obligations which I have described were not simply a distasteful burden imposed by a communistic society. They may have weighed heavily on a poor man, but to the rich man they were almost the only opportunity of displaying his riches. I suggest that here, rather than in an undeveloped sense of individual property, lies an explanation of the general acceptance of the obligation of lavish giving which rested on the wealthy. Where the whole range of material goods is so narrow, the social prestige that can be won by generosity, and the public demonstration of superiority which is made whenever gifts are given on the rich man's scale, bulk very large relatively to the advantages to be derived from the possession and use of the same goods. Such intangible satisfactions, after all, are not unknown in our own individualistic culture. We see their influence when the poor man gives his wife a lovely funeral, the rich man his daughter a lovely wedding, the millionaire endows a hospital or a university.

With us they play a relatively smaller part compared with the accumulation of the almost infinite variety of material goods that our economic technique can provide. Social emulation is directed very much more to acquisition, for each grade in the hierarchy of wealth has its own standard of possessions, and only at a very high level can the seeker after prestige afford to earn it by parting with his wealth on a large scale. In a word, competition in the acquisition of material goods is a more obvious and widespread feature of our society than is rivalry in munificence. Both forms of competition are equally individualistic; their relative importance in different cultures probably depends upon the possibility of rivalry in acquisition.

Perhaps this analysis may give a clue to what is really happening among the native societies which are now feeling for the first time the full force of European economic penetration. What has been changed is not their attitude towards property as such but their opportunities of acquisition and their standard of values. European contact has increased the value set on the possession of European goods to a point where this entirely outweighs the prestige that was formerly attached to generosity. It has made the observance of obligations unnecessary because economic ambitions can be satisfied without it. The education which it has brought with it stresses the right of the individual to enjoy the fruits of his own effort, and deliberately discountenances those claims of kindred to share in one another's good fortune which used to be taken for granted.

The result has been not to develop individual ambitions which formerly did not exist, but to turn such ambitions into new directions, and by doing so, in most cases, to throw the social mechanism seriously out of gear. The modern system of wage-earning or production for profit, whichever it may be, certainly allows individual merit to make its mark by the objective test of economic returns—if you accept the assumption that economic efficiency is the supreme merit. It also divorces economic, and therefore also social, advancement from the social responsibilities with which it was formerly bound up. This disappearance of social control over economic advancement cuts two ways. On the one hand, an industrious man can prosper now even if his chief has a spite against him. But on the other, there is no longer any reward for the exercise of socially approved qualities. The community as a whole no longer turns the ambitions of its members to advantage—except in the sense in which any increase in total production is held automatically to benefit the whole community.

A full analysis of the forces which are tending towards the disruption of Ganda village life would involve the discussion of many other than economic factors, and would lead me outside the scope of this paper. But there is one other important aspect of the separation of economic privilege from social obligation which needs to be considered. Such a separation—or else the mere disregard of traditional claims on superior wealth as soon as more attractive uses for it appear —seems to be almost universal among primitive peoples when they are brought into contact with European trade and initiated into the use of money. In the Ganda its peculiar form is due to a deliberate act of administrative intervention—the allocation to the chiefs in freehold tenure of the land over which they exercised authority at the time of the Uganda Agreement. This measure, by fixing the existing distribution in perpetuity, rendered the chiefs' economic position independent of any of the services which they formerly rendered to the king, such as the administration of justice or the organisation of public works.

Next these chiefs ceased even to be expected to render such services. They were persuaded to retire from office and replaced by younger, educated men, or when they died their official position was filled by a stranger, while their land passed to their heirs. Thus the landlord had no longer to render any return to superior authority for his privileged position—apart from a very low tax. In his relation with his inferiors—who now became tenants paying rent—a certain standard of leniency was imposed by the fact that there was plenty of land available, and they could leave him if they were dissatisfied. Some of the first generation of landlords kept up the old paternal relationship with their tenants. But when cotton was introduced, many of them made such heavy exactions on the yield of the peasants' crops that their dues had eventually to be limited by law, and none of this came back in any form to the tenants. It was devoted entirely to the personal uses of the landlord, who bought a motor car, sent his children to school, built a two-storied house in the capital, or perhaps visited Europe. One founded a native newspaper. Now, though the standard of exaction is fixed, the number of landlords who insist on their full rights is increasing, and the ingenuity which they show in interpreting the law in their favour is considerable. Many of them do not live on their land, but in the capital, and it is only through the collection of rent that they come into even indirect contact with their tenants. There is no longer any question of the peasants looking to them for personal assistance, and the moral obligation on the landlord to devote some of his returns to the improvement of the land itself which is recognised by European tradition is quite undreamt of. The peasant's ambition now is not to become a chief, but to buy his own piece of land and be independent of the landlord's claims.

In this particular case the introduction of the European standard of values has been accompanied by deliberate measures whose effect was to free economic privilege from the duties which formerly attached to it. But even where the process has not been assisted in this way, we find that obligations begin to be disregarded where they compete with the claims of the new standard of attainment in the matter of personal possessions. With the Ganda themselves the bond of blood-brotherhood, with its duty of lending unlimited assistance to the partner, is said to be too onerous in these days, and certain ceremonies involving feasting and presentations are evaded 'because of the expense'. I quote native opinion in both cases. Cases could be cited from other peoples in Africa of chiefs whose tribute of grain used to be stored up against famine, and who now sell it to traders and spend the proceeds; in the South Seas of headmen who use their position of authority over the village coconut groves to stint the distribution of the fruit in customary gifts so that they may themselves trade them against European goods. On the other side, subjects now resent giving to public works time which they could spend working for their own profit.

What we are confronted with, then, in these societies is not a change from a communistic to an individualistic attitude towards property, but an alteration in the means by which property can be acquired and in the uses to which it is put. Its acquisition under modern conditions depends on relationships entirely outside the social group to which the individual belongs—with an employer, if he is a wage-earner, with a merchant if he is a cultivator. In that sense the individual is independent of his community. But this is not so much a question of freedom from claims which formerly hampered his efforts as of opportunities which previously did not exist. In the uses of wealth much greater emphasis is laid on the acquisition of personal possessions than on the prestige attached to generosity, and this tendency is increased by an education which aims at raising the native standard of living—the range of possessions which are regarded as necessities. It seems hardly necessary to point out that the higher this standard is, the less room will there be in the economic calculations of most individuals for the display of generosity; yet in the long run in this simple fact lies the essential difference between the African scale of values and our own.

The change has dislocated village life in various ways. The village is no longer self-contained, the centre of all the interests of its members, for their attention is now focused outside it in the economic pursuits which for most of them form the main business of life. Moreover, with the Ganda the modern land system results in the substitution for the village organised under a single chief or landlord of a number of small holders unconnected by any tie with their neighbours. The bond of dependence now no longer attaches the peasant either to the political chief or to the landlord. In the sense that the ties which bind a number of individuals into a community are all being loosened in different ways, Ganda village life is certainly becoming more individualistic and approximating more closely to the type of society in which we live, where social links extend in manifold directions over an immense field in which contiguity plays hardly any part. But when we describe our society as individualistic *par excellence*, we lose sight of the very great extent to which with us the lower value set on individual generosity is balanced by the redistribution of wealth through the impersonal mechanism of the state. The problem for the development of native societies is how they are to evolve a system that will meet the social needs which are no longer provided for in the traditional way, and one of the main questions of policy ought to be how this evolution can be guided.

III

CHIEFTAINSHIP IN MODERN AFRICA

The contemporary development of African chieftainship is a question of considerable practical importance. The attitude which it will adopt towards the native chief in his relations with his own people is one of the major questions of policy which every colonial government has to decide. Some hold that a native society can only be satisfactorily ruled by—or through (the words are not quite synonymous)—its traditional head; others that the first duty of the civilising power is to free its native subjects from the oppression and tyranny of their own rulers; others make it their aim to steer a middle course, and preserve the native authority in his traditional position while adapting his functions to the requirements of the present day. All have in fact considerably altered by their mere presence both the nature and the basis of the chief's authority.

Yet they have so far been content with a very incomplete knowledge of the political systems which they uphold or condemn. To the advocates of Indirect Rule, it is the sanctity of tradition that creates the claim to obedience, and for that reason the traditional chief is the ideal instrument for moulding native society in the form that civilisation demands; to its opponents, authority in native societies on one-sided privileges maintained by the arbitrary use of force. Neither school of thought recognises that such an institution as the chieftainship depends for its maintenance on a complex series of relationships which cannot be reduced to a single attribute. Thus, those who are for destroying it ignore altogether the question of the considerations of their own advantage which prompt the subjects to accede to the chief's claims upon them; while those who wish to preserve it are often in danger of overlooking the degree to which modern circumstances are changing its nature.

There are before us then two complementary questions—what were the forces in native society which made the chief's power effective, and in what sphere did he exercise that power? That it consisted, not only in exacting the performance of duties from his subjects, but also in rendering services to them, is, I would suggest, the key to a real understanding of this institution both in its normal working and in the distortion which it has undergone in modern times. I propose to develop this theory in connexion with the chieftainship as it exists, and has existed, in Central and Southern Africa.

One might summarise the sources of the chief's authority by saying that it depended in part only on the supernatural sanctions attached to his heredity and in part on the due performance of his functions. By this I do not mean to suggest that any failure or abuse was instantly met by revolt and deposition, but rather that there was sufficient flexibility in the relations between governor and governed for discontent to make itself felt in ways which it was against the ruler's interest to disregard, while there were in practice often considerable checks on the abuse, of an authority which was in theory absolute.

In the area with which I am concerned the functions of the chief might be of three kinds, magical, political, and economic, and his privileges can be closely correlated with the exercise of these functions. Everywhere the paramount chief or king is believed to stand in a special relationship to the land, and in virtue of this relationship he is frequently responsible for the performance of rites upon which the fertility of the land depends and which only he can satisfactorily carry out. It is especially in connexion with these magical duties that his hereditary position, linking him as it does with the spirits of his predecessors, is of importance in validating his authority. Where the chief stands in this unique relationship to the supernatural powers which control the fortunes of his people, he might seem to hold all the trumps. Yet, in at least two tribes where this is the case, anthropological inquiry has found that in the political field his actions are circumscribed by the existence of councils of various kinds in which he does not hold a preponderant position, and whose authority is equal to his own.[1] Such facts emphasise the importance of looking for the source of political power not in the person of some individual who may seem to possess certain attributes of supremacy, but in the whole system which works to make authority effective in those spheres where authority is required.

The king's hereditary status is certainly an element in maintaining respect for his authority even where, as with the Ganda, he has no magical powers. Here his connexion by descent with the mythological founder of the kingdom at the same time justified his claim to absolute ownership of the country and everything in it and guaranteed his adherence to the tradition which was formally reasserted at his accession—a tradition which, it is worth mentioning, laid down not only the supremacy of the king but his duty to respect certain rights of his subjects.

But tradition and mythology remain as ultimate rather than immediate sanctions for obedience to authority. It is not to them that we must look for the bases of the everyday acceptance of the chief's position and performance of the subjects' duties. That is to be found rather in the reciprocal nature of their relationship—in the interpretation of the subjects' duties as returns for benefits received. I do not mean to suggest that this was a conscious attitude, still less that tribute or labour were rendered out of spontaneous gratitude, but rather that the maintenance of political authority carried with it advantages to the governed sufficient to make them acquiesce in the burdens which it imposed upon them.

What were these advantages? They vary of course with the exact nature of the political organisation in question. I can only speak in

[1] I refer to the Swazi and Bemba, who have been investigated by Dr. P. J. Schoeman and Dr. Audrey Richards respectively.

detail of the tribe which I know at first hand, the Ganda. With them the political functions of the chiefs, who formed a hierarchy appointed by the king and dependent for their position on his pleasure, consisted mainly in the administration of justice and the organisation of warfare. I have myself heard an old peasant say that God showed the Ganda especial favour in giving them chiefs to settle their quarrels. Warfare with them went beyond the mere organisation of defence, in itself a service of some importance, to constitute, in the form of raids on neighbouring tribes, a speedier way of increasing their material possessions than any more conventionally economic activity.

In economic matters authority might seem at first sight to have carried with it a position of pure privilege. In the first place, the subject's right to occupy land, and hence his entire livelihood, depended theoretically on the king and practically on the chief to whose village he attached himself. For failure to render the customary services, as for any other action displeasing to the chief, he was liable to eviction. Those who see in African chieftainship nothing but arbitrary tyranny may seem to find here an argument for their point of view, but for an analysis of the working of the institution what is relevant is that the services rendered by the peasant are not given in a one-sided submission to supernatural power or physical force, but in return for rights of fundamental importance. To the Ganda there was no injustice in the fact that these rights were not unconditional. Moreover, he had a ready means of expressing dissatisfaction with his chief by moving to another village, and since the chief's economic privileges gave him a motive for desiring to attract and retain a large following, this right was an effective check on tyrannous behaviour. At the same time, the chief's rights of eviction and of physical punishment certainly were an element in securing the obedience of his followers.

The rights which a chief could claim from his subjects consisted of a gourd of beer in every brew, a considerable portion of the goods paid over in compensation for any offence tried by him, and services when required in the building of his houses and the fence which surrounded them. He received also his share of the taxes collected through his agency at the command of the king, and on the return from a raiding expedition it rested with him to distribute among his followers that portion of the spoil captured by them which was left when the king had selected his share and, of course, to retain as much of it as he thought fit.

But this system did not mean a constantly increasing accumulation of wealth in the hands of the privileged few, for the simple reason that in the native economy satiation point was reached early, and when it was reached the rich man turned from the enjoyment of possession to the enjoyment of munificence. Generosity was expected of a chief and was the best way to increase his following; and on the size of his following depended wealth, prestige, and promotion to the control over a wider area. Among other peoples the accumulation of

34

wealth in the chief's hands has been found to serve even more obvious social needs in an even more direct and obvious way, for example in forming a reserve against famine or providing for the maintenance of a standing army.

This very summary account of the relations between chief and people in Ganda society indicates the mutual dependence which formed the basis of the native political organisation. To the peasant the chief was the ultimate source of his livelihood and a more immediate source of material benefits; he also represented the authority and leadership necessary for orderly relations in peace and the successful organisation of war. To the chief his followers brought wealth and prestige provided he dealt fairly with them—a proviso which shows how the institution contained within itself checks on the abuse of a privileged position.

A further check existed in the system of succession. The hereditary principle did not mean that certain individuals were destined by birth alone to succeed to authority. There was always a certain range of choice, which made it worth while for persons who lusted for power to show themselves fit for it. Any son of the king might be selected to succeed him; while in the case of a chief the choice was even wider, extending to the sons of his brothers: moreover, under the Ganda system in which chiefs could be transferred by the king from one district to another, a chief's heir did not necessarily succeed to the dead man's position. If this was important, a more experienced man might be appointed to it while the young heir was given a smaller village until his merit was tried.

A feature of the Ganda system which again limited the action both of the king and the chiefs was the existence, side by side with the theoretically supreme authority, of a counsellor whose influence carried very great weight. While the heir could dismiss his father's counsellor, he was not normally expected to do so; so that the new holder of any political position, from the king downwards, usually entered upon his office subject to the advice of an older and more experienced man. This counsellor's advice was asked before any drastic step was taken, such as the deposition of a chief by the king or the eviction of a peasant by the chief; and in the case of the chiefs he was the recognized channel through which peasants who considered that they were unfairly treated could express their grievances.

In describing this system I have not been guided by any sentimental desire to idealise a vanished past. I do not mean to present it as incapable of improvement or to suggest that the principles of government which European powers have set themselves to introduce have no advantages. Clearly it left room for many acts of oppression against individual subjects and gave to the rulers a wider scope for the indulgence of personal feelings and desires than Europeans in theory approve. I have been careful to say, not that the system prevented the abuse of power, but that it set limits to such abuse. Can we say more of the political institutions of the most advanced civilisations? They have their abuses, too, which seem less flagrant perhaps only because they are more familiar. The main aim of my analysis, however, has been to try to give a more complete picture than that usually painted of a native system of government in operation, and by doing so to indicate the kind of phenomena which ought to be taken into account by those who set out to modify such systems, particularly if their aim is to utilise them as part of an organisation on European lines. Indirect Rule has been defined as the progressive adaptation of native institutions to modern conditions; but I have suggested already that many administrations which purport to have adopted Indirect Rule have not looked beyond one single factor in the native institutions concerned, namely the hereditary principle. Some have supposed that by merely preserving the hereditary principle they have fully respected all native rights; others have believed that provided they employ for the purpose an hereditary authority they can induce natives to obey any orders, however burdensome or unwelcome, that the European government may decide to issue.

This rather superficial conception of the nature of chieftainship has resulted in a general failure to recognise that the entire basis of the chief's position has been altered by the very advent of European government. What was in many areas one of the most important functions of the supreme authority has been completely removed. I mean the organisation of war, which in some African societies has justified a system of government much more autocratic than that which I have described among the Ganda. Even where he has retained his judicial authority the modern chief has lost the right to inflict severe punishments for offences against himself. Where new systems of land tenure have been introduced the fundamental economic relationship between chief and people is broken. Christianity and the obsolescence of public ritual have affected this relationship on the religious side. On the other side, authority rests now, not on popularity or on the rendering of specific services to the governed, but on the power of the European government, which, though it may remove chiefs from office, seldom does so for the reasons which would cause native opinion to desire such a step. It is for this reason—because it has put the chief out of reach of the sanctions with which he had formerly to reckon—that a government which maintains his authority without understanding its real nature may well be condoning abuses of it which could not in the past have been committed with impunity. Moreover, modern economic conditions create the possibility of abuses which could not in the past have been committed at all. The possibilities of turning one's economic privileges to direct personal advantage are now unlimited; yet the most superficially literal conception of Indirect Rule involves the maintenance of the chief's traditional privileges. Because they have dissociated these privileges from the corresponding responsibilities, those in authority have sometimes failed to see that under modern conditions tribute paid to chiefs is coming to be just that one-sided burden that it was sometimes thought to have been before. Yet these same conditions make any effective protest out of the question.

This is one way in which the nature of the chief's position as one part of a reciprocal relationship has been misunderstood. The possibilities of the other party—his subjects as a body, or any one of them —retaliating for his failure to do his due part have been removed; for it is only those who reject government through the chief altogether and propose to replace it by democracy on European lines, who have concerned themselves with the subjects' point of view, and they only misinterpret it by forgetting again that the subject had rights as well as duties. By removing the checks on the chief's action at the same time that they converted his payment in kind into a money payment, European administrations have shown that in the long run traditional sentiments and ethical standards do not prevail where the ruler has a clear interest in disregarding them, and perhaps that such standards do not even appear to be applicable in a situation so new as that created by the presence of the European trader on the one hand, and on the other by the accumulation in the chief's possession, not of cattle, maize-cobs, beer, or garments, but of that currency with which European goods can be obtained.

At the same time that they have altered the basis of the chief's authority in a way which tips the balance of power in his favour, even though he may no longer be able to assert himself by the use of physical violence, European governments have assigned to him many duties which did not form part of his functions before.[2] Some of these, such as the collection of census figures, enforcement of regulations for the destruction of old cotton plants, encouragement of such activities as the killing of rats, might be described as neutral in their effect on the relation between chief and subject. But others, those which involve the use of the chief's authority in calling upon his subjects to enter upon distasteful and arduous pursuits which bring them no apparent advantage and throw out of gear the whole routine of their lives, inevitably produce a complete distortion of that relationship. I refer, of course, to the use of the chief in obtaining labour for European employers, or recruits in those colonies where conscription is in force, in collecting taxes imposed by the government, and sometimes in enforcing the cultivation by natives of commercial crops. Where these are among the duties of the chief, he is simply an instrument of the superior government and is plainly recognised by the natives as such. It may be true that his prestige and generally dominant position gains him an obedience which an agent sent from outside would not obtain without resort to actual force, but it is quite mistaken to interpret this as meaning that the hereditary status of the chief justifies his every action in his subjects' eyes, and to conclude that in order to satisfy European interests without disintegrating native society, it is sufficient to make the chief their mouthpiece. The

[2] This situation is admirably described by Professor N. De Cleene in his article 'Les Chefs indigènes au Mayombe', *Africa*, vol. viii, no. 1, p. 70.

natives may continue to obey, but the chieftainship ceases to be a native institution, and they are as well aware of that fact as any anthropologist.

This last interpretation of Indirect Rule is one which would never be accepted by the original exponent of a theory whose basic principle is that the development of native society must not be subservient to the demands of the European market. But it contains elements that are also present in the popular attitude towards Indirect Rule sincerely conceived as the best vehicle for such a development. Here again it is argued that civilisation can be made acceptable if it is introduced through the chief, and again the argument is only a half-truth. It is true that the prestige of the chief often leads his subjects to imitate him in following European ways. Christianity itself has sometimes been adopted in this manner, not always without sudden mass conversion from one sect to another. But for the chief's example to be effective, the innovation must be in something which is either a matter of indifference to the people or else appears to offer them some positive advantage. And further, the apparent advantages may not always be consistent with the effective working of the complex of native institutions taken as a whole. It is just as easy for progress to become synonymous with disruption if an hereditary chief is made its apostle as it is where the native who claims to have become civilised is encouraged to reject the chief's authority—though the process of disruption may be less obvious.

I am not meaning to suggest that Indirect Rule is a chimera, that in modern conditions the chieftainship has gone through such changes that it is no longer recognisable as an African institution at all and might as well give place to something more efficient and more consonant with modern theories of government. On the contrary, I hold that the future of African society depends upon the success with which continuity and its attendant stability can be maintained in the process of transition which it is now passing through. My argument is that the link which unites the chief with his ancestors is not by itself strong enough to bind the present to the past: that what is needed is a full understanding in every case of what chieftainship has meant and what it can mean in terms of authority and leadership. Certainly it has to acquire a new meaning, for the spheres in which leadership is demanded are no longer the same; the emphasis has shifted from the waging of war to the construction of public works, and the redistribution of revenues received is now a matter not of personal generosity but of budgetary expenditure.

The fundamental necessity for the constructive development of native administration is, as I have suggested, an understanding, not only of the nature of the claim to authority, but of the reasons why authority was in fact obeyed and above all the duties which authority involved. Such an understanding would give a sounder basis than the chance of administrative convenience for the modifications in the chief's status which modern circumstances render necessary. It would make it possible to meet the criticism that Indirect Rule means the maintenance of obsolete tyrannies by the power of alien arms, by curtailing those privileges which, divorced from the responsibility which formerly accompanied them, have in fact become tyrannous. It would dispel the illusion that chiefs can be made the instruments of interests inimical to those of their own people and native political organisation remain intact; and the more insidious illusion that in regions where native society has been systematically reduced to dependence on wage-labour for European employers it can be recreated by allotting major administrative functions to hereditary chiefs.

With this understanding there must go a recognition that the chieftainship is not in any society an isolated phenomenon but one of a group of interdependent institutions which combine to determine its sphere of influence. The commands of a native chief are as constitutional as those of a modern parliament—in the sense that he takes for granted the whole social organisation of which he is a part. Arbitrary as his power may be in personal matters, it is exercised within the limits of a traditional system of law which it is his duty to uphold and not to modify.

Thus when he is invited by the European government to throw his weight on the side of an innovation desired by them, it is not as an autocrat whose word is law that he makes his influence effective, but either as their recognised instrument or as a person whose general prestige entitles his counsels to respect. Indeed, the belief that fundamental alterations in the structure of any society could be made by a mere word of command rests on a quite unreal conception of the nature of authority and of society itself.

The next step that needs to be taken, in the constructive interpretation of Indirect Rule, is an appreciation of the chieftainship as part of this complex whole which will enable those responsible to judge the value to the society concerned of the modifications which they propose to make through the agency of the native authority.[3] Given such an understanding this system could make possible a more satisfactory development of African society than it has sometimes achieved hitherto, and could refute some of the criticisms brought against it by those most interested in native welfare.

[3] An admirable study of native political institutions from this point of view has been made by Messrs. Gordon Brown and Bruce Hutt in their volume, *Anthropology In Action: An Experiment in the Iringa District of the Iringa Province, Tanganyika Territory*, Oxford University Press, for the International Institute of African Languages and Cultures, London, 1935.

IV

THE ANTHROPOLOGIST'S APPROACH TO NATIVE EDUCATION

It would be a mistake to suppose that the contribution of the anthropologist to the problem of native education must be limited to a description of the traditional system of the people in question. The education which is given by Europeans to native children is regarded, and rightly, as the most potent element in the process of transformation which native societies must undergo if they are ever to cope successfully with the demands which modern conditions make upon them. It is perforce given in an entirely new way, which as a matter of practical necessity often involves removing the pupil from his normal environment to a life which at the best is artificial. Moreover, the modern educationist is trained in a science which devotes itself to the study of methods of imparting knowledge, and only the most fanatical admirer of native culture could suggest that he is likely to have anything to learn from the African parent in that respect.

The interest of the anthropologist is not so much in education in the narrowly pedagogic sense but in the part which it can play in the adaptation of native culture to changed conditions. It is because he claims that his science can interpret native society in a way which indicates what innovations from outside can be assimilated by it, and where a sound basis can be found for developments, that the anthropologist offers his services to the practical man.

Here, then, his task is two-fold. He can show where modern educational institutions cause unnecessary dislocation in the lives of the families whose children pass through them, and, from what he knows of the life that the adult native will have to lead, he can draw conclusions as to the type of education which will be of most real value to him.

Under the first head the anthropologist would consider such subjects as children's household duties, their instruction in native crafts and native tradition, and their obligations to relatives within and outside the immediate family circle.

The school must take the child from his home for a considerable proportion of the day and year. This inevitably means a removal of the child from the sphere of paternal discipline—such as it is. Many Europeans would claim as an advantage of the school that it gives a training in obedience, regularity, and so on, which is entirely lacking in the native home; and in the sense that behaviour which would be dealt with severely by a European parent goes unnoticed in the native household, this is true. But it is not fair to make this indictment without looking for the ways in which the native child does receive that minimum of training in his duties as a member of society which he evidently must acquire somehow. In so far as this comes from mere association with his parents and other older people, from their casual comments on his behaviour and that of others, with perhaps instruction how to act in a given situation as it happens to arise, he must lose it to the extent that he is out of his parents' reach; the school can only provide, in school-hours, its own discipline suited to its own purposes. But it is worth while to look for more concretised educational agencies and see whether the school cannot co-operate with them rather than merely disregard anything that conflicts with a standardised time-table. The small household duties that fall to native children obviously help to train them both in responsibility and in the requirements of family co-operation; and where the school unnecessarily makes their performance difficult and thus comes to be made an excuse for their neglect, it is deliberately acting as a disruptive force. There is no reason, for instance, why village schools should not arrange their hours so that the girls can help at home in the preparation of the midday meal. On the other hand, some types of duty are perhaps altogether incompatible with organised European education; an example is the Basuto custom whereby boys are sent to herd cattle at distant posts for months at a time. Yet even here, since it seems that they prefer the cattle post to the school, the question suggests itself whether some curriculum could not be devised that would fit into the period when they are in the villages.

It is important to know, too, whether absence at school is going to mean that the child grows up actually lacking in skill or knowledge which is essential to his participation in the adult life of his village. This is admittedly unlikely, but it is a consideration which ought to be borne in mind. It is here that the question of instruction in native crafts is relevant. Where this is given by father to son it has the functions, over and above its utilitarian value, of binding these two in co-operation and of impressing the child with respect for the father's superior knowledge. Instruction in native crafts in school can only fulfil the utilitarian function. They will not in any case be practised unless there is a demand for the product, and, while their preservation often has an aesthetic value, it will only be believed to maintain the continuity of tradition by people who have never seriously inquired in what the handing on of tradition consists.

A very important factor in education is the ceremonial in which kinship obligations are formally expressed on the occasion of various events of family life, and, above all, of death. To the anthropologist it would seem that educational authorities should show all possible leniency in allowing their pupils to attend such ceremonies, since refusal to do so is encouraging the child to flout the bonds of kinship in their most sacred form. The schoolmaster may retort that this advice is hopelessly impractical—that no child can afford to be away from school for months on end as some mortuary ritual demands. He would obviously be right; yet the anthropologist could answer that sympathetic inquiry would probably reveal the possibility of a compromise that native feeling would accept as satisfactory. In Buganda, for example, it used to be incumbent on the immediate relatives of a deceased person to sleep in his house all through the period of mourning, but it is now recognised as sufficient for any one who is in regular employment to come home only for the two nights of the final ceremony.

Lastly, we must consider the question of initiation rites, in so far as they constitute a system of education. There is no doubt that in many cases the initiation period includes among other elements the training and instruction of the candidates by their elders, and if that instruction was found in a particular case to contain elements which were of value from the point of view of native life but did not form part of the ordinary school curriculum, an educational authority which did nothing to replace them would, by anthropological standards, be failing in its duty. It is possible that the method which has been tried at Malangali school, Tanganyika, of inviting tribal elders to come regularly and talk to the boys of their own people, might to some extent replace this function of the initiation period, at any rate for types of instruction which it is not thought essential to give secretly; this is merely a tentative suggestion. It is also important to point out that the sex instruction which was given at initiation schools was not, as is so often said, a mere encouragement to licence. Those who make that criticism forget that the initiation period always involves a rigid seclusion from the opposite sex. Moreover, the instruction included as an essential element the inculcation of the rules regulating sexual behaviour, and in most cases covered such subjects as the care of the wife during pregnancy.

So far I have been concerned with the question of the inevitable breach which the school must make in the continuity of native life, and with suggestions for keeping that breach from growing wider than it need be. I must now turn to the second part of my task—the attempt to indicate what type of education would seem, from the anthropologist's point of view, best suited to the needs of a modern native society. For this purpose education must be considered as having two aspects—the imparting of a body of knowledge and the inculcation of a sense of values. Theories regarding the type of knowledge which should be imparted have tended up till now to be confined to generalisations which have not always produced the most satisfactory results in practice. It is accepted that the purpose of education is to fit the pupil for life, and above all to increase the potential value of his existence both to his community and to himself. It is often stated that its aim in democratic countries is to 'give him every opportunity', and the meaning of the phrase is too often taken for granted. What is actually implicit in it, in Europe, is the theory that nobody should be debarred by poverty from a training which will enable him, if he is intelligent enough, to enter some profession which carries with it social prestige or a large income. Too often the same conception has been transplanted to the colonies, where it becomes the justification for an educational system directed almost exclusively to qualifying natives for employment in European enterprises or in the service of their own or the European government. Now there is everything to be said for training natives to practise professions for which the development of their community creates a need; but since the numbers engaged in this way must always be a minority, the question arises whether the best *general* education is one which is devised with a view to their needs.

It is true that the European system may be said to be based on this principle. All education is conceived as culminating in the university, and the pupil whose attainments are not sufficient to make it worth his while to complete the whole course drops out after the elementary or the secondary school as the case may be. But in this country at least dissatisfaction is beginning to be felt with such a system, and it is coming to be recognised that the pupil whose abilities are not primarily intellectual requires a training on altogether different lines. How much more must this be true of an African society, where the difference is so much greater between the village life which will be the lot of the majority and the alien existence in a European environment to which the minority hope, and are encouraged, to aspire.

The anthropologist, looking at education as a potential means of developing native society *as a whole*, rather than as a method of removing certain individuals from that society to an alien environment where they as individuals may earn prestige and pecuniary gain, feels that it should have a direct bearing on the life that will in fact be the lot of the majority of the pupils who pass through it. To him a satisfactory system would be one which did not hold out escape from his native surroundings as the reward of the good scholar, but was directed to make life there more agreeable and more interesting. He would admit also that European education must make village life profitable, since to the natives the prospect of earning a good wage is the main inducement to school attendance.

What, then, is the type of education which he would recommend for the average pupil? Its guiding principle would be that every subject in the curriculum must have a demonstrable bearing on the needs of village life. Agriculture and hygiene would be the most important subjects, and the teaching of agriculture would be guided by a knowledge of native methods that would take into account the possibility that these methods might be better suited to local soils and climate than others imported from Europe, would see where improvements in technique would be practicable with existing native appliances and means of co-operation, and would aim throughout at adapting what exists rather than attempting to draw an entirely new system on a clean slate.[1] Handicrafts could be taught of a type for which there would be a demand in a village whose standard of living

[1] Messrs. Faulkner and Mackie in their book, *West African Agriculture* (1933), give some very interesting examples of cases where traditional methods have been the most satisfactory in view of local circumstances, and where attempts to introduce profitable crops have failed because their cultivation could not be assimilated to the general economic calendar.

was rising. Carpentry and joinery could be linked up with efforts to popularise more hygienic ways of building with native materials, as has been done at Malangali school. There is probably now hardly any African village where a tailor would not be a valuable member of the community. To be able to solder pots and pans and to mend bicycles is an accomplishment which, in Uganda at least, could always be turned to account.

As for the literary side of education, the value of the three R's and of an elementary knowledge of the official language of the colony is obvious. But I see no reason why this official language should be taught in any other way than that in which a foreign language would be taught in a modern European school. Its value to the native is for convenience in travelling and in intercourse with persons who cannot speak his own language. I leave out of account for the moment the question of those who wish to enter skilled European employment, since, as I have indicated, they require their own specialised training. Over and above this utilitarian value, the native is immensely interested in learning facts about other parts of the world, and this I suggest should be the starting-point of the cultural aspects of education. He wants to be able to read newspapers, though he would certainly prefer to have newspapers in his own language, and his curiosity as regards the subjects which would be included in an intelligent treatment of geography is unbounded. But his interest in the treasures of a foreign literature is a negative quantity, and time spent in teaching him advanced English so that these may be revealed to him is time lost. I make this assertion in no supercilious spirit, for I believe it to be true of the vast majority of the pupils of any European school. Of course, it is true that each European nation has its own imaginative literature. But one cannot supply the lack of it in Africa by an imported product; the only thing to do is to wait till Africa evolves its own.

This, then, is the type of education which an anthropologist would recommend as a suitable preparation of the African for village life. It puts practical considerations first, but I hope it is not open to the accusation that it involves disregarding the intellectual development of the African and denying him those features of our civilisation which we prize most highly. The question whether a wider mental horizon is an unmixed blessing can be left to psychologists and philosophers; certainly it is universally assumed that education ought to produce it, and so long as this assumption is made it would be clearly unjust that African education should abandon this aim. I simply suggest that it can only be effectively achieved by making the new knowledge that we impart to the African centre upon the type of question that he is himself asking.

For the exceptional pupil who is capable of entering the government service or a profession, it is clear that a wholly different type of education is required; and so long as examinations set in London or Paris are made the standard of attainment all over the world it is useless to talk of local modifications. To his problems anthropological knowledge has nothing to contribute; it merely suggests that the needs of the majority ought not to be subordinated to his.

Lastly we come to the question of the values which are inculcated, directly or indirectly, through the system of education. The anthropologist here would utter a warning against the acceptance of an absolute standard of values, except perhaps in the limited field where certain values can be shown to have been universally accepted. To him values grow out of, and reinforce, the functioning of systems of social co-operation; so that the educationist who takes upon himself to imbue his pupils with a new standard ought to consider how far the condemnation of actions formerly approved, or the encouragement of behaviour that used not to be permissible, will affect the smooth running of these systems. If, as is the case with the missionary, he regards himself as bound to introduce a new ethical code, he should at least do so with his eyes open, aware of the dislocation which he will cause and alert to devise means of mitigating it. This applies, of course, particularly to the Christian code of sexual ethics. The anthropologist would warn him, too, that while it is easy to overthrow regulations which run counter to normal human desires, it is by no means as easy to introduce new prohibitions.

There is another aspect of the problem of values which has so far received very little consideration. Europeans frequently claim to have invented 'individualism'. They regard the more backward peoples as having been, till their advent, debarred from 'progress' by the shackles of communal ownership and kinship obligations which made it impossible for individual labour or enterprise to reap its due reward. Such a view can only rest on a very superficial view of a primitive community. Such studies as those of Professor Malinowski have shown how much individual rivalry exists among the peoples who are most unlike the stock pictures of 'economic man', and his conclusions could be paralleled from other fields. It is quite true that there are certain cases where obligations suited to a different economic system weigh heavily and sometimes unjustly on natives anxious to adopt modern methods, and these cases call for remedies designed to meet the actual circumstances. But an education which stresses solely the commercialising of all possessions and the right of the individual to the fruits of his own efforts, and encourages resistance to the claims that were formerly respected, overlooks the fact that every society recognises some form of mutual responsibility for those of its members who cannot, and even sometimes for those who will not, work. At some stages this responsibility has rested on the Church; in modern societies it rests on the State; in primitive communities it is made effective through the system of kinship obligations. An educational policy which deliberately sets out to break that system down ought at least to cast about for something to put in its place.

45

V

MODERN DEVELOPMENTS IN AFRICAN LAND TENURE

African land tenure is a subject so vast that in dealing with it one hesitates to commit oneself to statements of general application lest particular instances should be found to controvert them. Yet, when it is considered from the point of view of culture change, it is possible to discern a number of general trends, the nature of which is similar because their cause is the same—the impact on African society of the commercial economy of Western Europe with its infinite range of forms of wealth and possibilities of acquiring them. Though other forces too are active in the modern process of culture change, this is the most pervasive, and its influence can be traced in the development of every institution. In the case of land rights, closely bound up as they are with systems of production, the influence is direct and obvious.

The Indigenous Systems

Certain very broad generalisations may also be hazarded concerning the indigenous systems of the agricultural peoples. In the first place, these systems were appropriate to a subsistence economy, where people obtained the goods they needed almost entirely by the work of their own hands, exploiting the resources of their immediate environment. In such an economy there could be no commodity more valuable than land, no circumstance in which it would be profitable to dispose of land. Land, in short, had no exchange value. Certain writers ascribe to African peoples an abstract theory of the sacredness of land which inhibits their recognition of its economic potentialities. Th. Heyse, for example, writes: 'It would be contrary to progress to seek to keep alive in the native mind the idea that the land is inalienable because it belongs to the living and dead in common.'[1]

The mythical charter, as Malinowski calls it, of rights in land, the conception of it as the home of the ancestor spirits, and the idea that to dispose of it is sacrilege,[2] are indeed common features of African societies. Some of them also express in proverbial form the conception that the land must be preserved for coming generations. Yet there are not many recorded cases where someone who was invited to dispose of land for a profitable consideration has invoked such principles as a ground for refusal, though it is true that some of the chiefs who made the earliest agreements to alienate land were not fully aware what they were doing. When circumstances arise in which land can pass out of the hands of the group with a traditional claim to it, their reluctance to see this happen is formulated in terms of

[1] *Grandes Lignes du Régime des Terres au Congo Belge,* 1947, p. 17.
[2] Cf. M. Fortes, *Dynamics of Clanship among the Tallensi,* 1945, p. 178.

46

responsibility towards the dead or the unborn. Yet it would surely be unrealistic to conceive of these ideas as the primary reason why the right to alienate land is not commonly found in African custom; more fundamental is the absence of any motive for its exercise

Secondly, two factors set limits to the amount of land which any individual would seek to utilise. Here the basic limitation was that imposed by technique; where the only implement known is the hoe, no one can clear much more ground than his neighbours. But, if he could, the second factor would come into play—that there was no incentive to cultivate more land than was necessary to provide an adequate food supply.

The level of technique also influenced the system of land rights in that, in the absence of any knowledge of manuring (and often even of livestock), the fertility of the soil could only be maintained by shifting cultivation; either the whole village was moved, or cultivation alternated with fallow in an area surrounding a group of permanent habitations. In the first case no permanent rights were acquired in any particular piece of land; in the second and more common, however, rights of occupation in an area large enough to allow for fallowing were normally acquired.

These then are the limitations set by circumstances to the development of African customary systems of land tenure. From the social point of view the essential common characteristic was that every individual had a right to the use of land derived, not from any economic transaction, but from his status either as a member of a kinship group or the subject of a political authority. The controlling authority of any settlement, whether a political chief or the head or elders of a kinship group, in the first instance allotted land to an applicant, whether a young man about to set up his household, or, in the case of a chief, any man who sought to attach himself to him. Once allotted, the land remained in his hands and passed to his heirs, and the original allocation was often large enough to maintain several generations of descendants. Thus sub-divisions of the settlement might be formed, looking to their own senior members as the relevant authorities for these units of land. The growing tendency of these sub-divisions to assert their independence of any wider authority is a feature of modern developments.

So long, however, as this wider authority was recognised, it had the right to reallocate land which was superfluous to the needs of any of its members. In addition, its consent was required for any transaction which conferred rights in the land of the group upon non-members of it. There were two principal ways in which this could be done. A man who was not using the whole area over which he had rights of cultivation might allot part of it to an outsider. The latter might be formally adopted into the group or ally himself with it by marriage, but if this was not done it was recognised that a member of the land-holding group would in case of need have a prior claim on the land. He was often expected to make a present at harvest-time to the right-holder on whose land he was living. Thus his position had points in common with that of a tenant, and the word is commonly used to describe such a person. But the essential difference between such an arrangement and the leasing of land as Europeans understand it was that it was not regarded by the right-holder as an economically profitable transaction. There was no question of turning to economic advantage land which he could not exploit directly or of calculation of payments in relation to economic potentialities; the advantage to the right-holder lay in the social prestige attaching to a man with dependants.[3]

The other way in which land rights could be transferred was by pledging land against a loan. Debts were most commonly incurred for the payment of fines or of bridewealth, or for the refund of bridewealth in case of divorce. Until the loan was repaid, the creditor was allowed to cultivate an agreed piece of land. Here again there was a fundamental difference from a modern mortgage in that, after no matter how long a period, the land could be redeemed by the repayment of the debt.

These were the general characteristics of the systems of land rights which the first Europeans found in Africa. To observers imbued with nineteenth-century ideas on 'the magic of property' their most striking feature appeared to be that the cultivator had in no case the absolute right to dispose as he pleased of his own land. Holding in addition the view that any form of government which was not a democracy must be a tyranny, such observers saw in the claims of African rulers to ultimate rights over the disposal of the land the justification of oppression against which the humble farmer must be defenceless, and pictured him in a state of constant insecurity, hardly able to count on reaping what he had sown. They did not realise that the features of the African system which appeared to them as defects would only be so in the context of a money economy, with the many opportunities that it offers of turning rights in land to profitable account. Hence, what seems at first sight a paradox, but is, in fact, no more than a logical development: modern conditions have created in Africa the very insecurity which early critics regarded as inherent in the indigenous system.

In the period of subsistence economy, however, one might say that, although there was a degree of political insecurity, there was little economic insecurity. That is to say, anyone who was held by a powerful chief to have flouted his authority was liable to severe punishment, which might involve expulsion and confiscation of property, if not execution. Undoubtedly the result of this was to make life precarious for those in the immediate entourage of powerful chiefs. But there were limits set to such arbitrary action by the fact that every chief desired a large following, and that few were so secure from rivals that they could afford to make themselves generally hated.

[3] Cf. *Report of the Committee on Native Land Tenures in Kikuyu Province*, 1933.

48

There was no question of depriving a cultivator of his land in order to turn it to greater profit. And where there was no powerful political authority this source of insecurity was not present at all.

New Factors In The Situation Today

Today the systems of land rights operate in different conditions. By far the most important new factor is the introduction of money, the acquisition of which opens up the possibility of an unlimited range of personal satisfactions. Land is no longer a unique commodity; it can be exchanged for money. Again, it is now profitable to cultivate land for other purposes than subsistence, and Africans everywhere are being actively encouraged to do so. From this two consequences follow.

In the first place nearly everyone is now cultivating more land, and since, at the same time, populations are increasing and soil fertility decreasing, and in some cases the available land has been limited by alienation policies, land has become a scarce commodity for which there is competition. In the second, there is competition for special types of land, of which cocoa farms in West Africa form the most conspicuous example.

In these circumstances the value of the consideration offered for the right to cultivate land will inevitably rise, and those who have the right to allocate it are not slow to turn this right to profitable account. The higher the value of the payment, the more anxious is the man who makes it to be secure in the rights which he has acquired; when his point of view is accepted and those granting the rights agree that they will assert no claims against him, the sale of land has begun, whether or not it is countenanced by the custodians of the law. In parts of West Africa the price of land sold outright is now twice the amount for which it could be pledged.[4]

Complementary to the man who sees where money can be made from the exercise of rights over land is he who needs money and has no other way of raising it than by the surrender of land rights.

This is the man who, in the eyes of early observers, was at so severe a disadvantage in that he had no secure title on which to raise capital for the improvement of his land. They sadly overrated the prudence of the husbandman, as they underrated the initiative of the moneylender. Though the heavy burden of debt that weighs upon the Gold Coast cocoa farmer has been incurred through the pledging of land or its produce, the sums that have been raised for productive purposes must be small indeed. A high proportion of the debt has been incurred in the attempt to keep up the standard of living that was adopted at the time when cocoa prices were at their maximum; of recent years it has been quite impossible for the majority of farmers to maintain this standard without borrowing.

An additional cause in this particular area is litigation over land claims, which has raged in the Gold Coast ever since gold prospectors

[4] C. K. Meek, *Land Law and Custom in the Colonies*, p. 159.

49

began to offer payment to chiefs for the grant of concessions. As soon as it became apparent that there was money to be made in this way, neighbours began to assert claims over land on their boundaries in which they had previously taken no interest, and such claims were fought in one court after another till the costs amounted to far more than any profit that could have been derived from the land in dispute. They were met, first by contributions from the persons concerned, and later by pledging the land, so that it was lost through sheer anxiety to claim it as a source of profit.

Along with the changes in circumstances which make it worth while for the farmer to increase the extent of his cultivation have come other changes which make it practicable. He can use the plough instead of the hoe and thus clear more ground himself; or he can employ the labour of men who are also alive to the attractions of money but are not in a position to acquire it by growing cash crops. One consequence of this is the reluctance of individuals or sub-divisions of a land-holding group to recognise the traditional rights of the heads of the group to redistribute surplus land; it is perhaps the principal motive in the assertion by these smaller units of their independence of outside control. Another is a tendency for those persons who have authority to allocate land to take advantage of it, either to secure large areas for themselves or to allot them in return for payment—in the latter case, explicitly recognising the transaction as a sale. Thirdly, right-holders find that their land may be made to yield more material satisfactions than the prestige derived from installing dependants upon it. Thus the position of the tenant today is really insecure; he may be evicted because the right-holder wants to plant wattle on the land where he grew his food crops, or even because he has planted it himself and the right-holder sees the way, by asserting his right of resumption, to secure to himself the resultant profit. The most striking instances of this type of development come from East Africa.[5]

The types of development so far described are changes in modes of dealing with land which result from the exercise of existing rights to land in new ways in response to new incentives. They create, both for the African societies concerned and for the governments responsible for their administration, the problem of deciding which of these new ways is to be regarded as legitimate; in other words, what type of transaction the courts will uphold. One aspect of the problem arises from the desire of governments to influence the direction of culture change towards ends which they consider socially desirable—above all, to prevent the destructive utilisation of land and its reckless alienation. Another comes from the fact that where land tenure is concerned, there is in every African society an opposition between those whose interests lie in the acceptance of new standards and those whose interests lie in the maintenance of the old. All kinds of cases occur where each side can put forward a claim that is entirely just

[5] See A. Phillips, *Report on Native Tribunals in Kenya*, 1945, passim.

in terms of the values which it accepts. Suppose pledged land is redeemed by an individual who has raised the redemption money by his unaided efforts. Should it return to the joint control of the group who pledged it, as custom would dictate? If the man who put up the money declares that he has no intention of surrendering control of land which, but for him, might never have been bought back, he has an argument which will command the sympathy of other commercially-minded Africans and of many Europeans.

Again, take the case of the tenant in a Kikuyu reserve. Most Europeans will agree with the old-fashioned African in condemning the sharp practice of the right-holder who evicts him to take his wattle plantation. But supposing the prior claim of the right-holding group is asserted in order to provide a holding for one of its members who has grown up in a squatter village in the settled area and decides to return to the reserve rather than enter into a labour tenancy, there may arise a conflict between two equally valid conceptions of justice. The youth has an admitted claim to a holding on the land of his kindred, but it is he now who is the stranger, compared with a tenant who may be farming the same land as his father and grandfather.

The solution will inevitably be found in the recognition of commercial transactions in land of the types known to European law, and measures to protect the weaker party—such as the recognition of a claim to compensation for unexhausted improvements—will doubtless be introduced on the advice of the governing authorities to temper the self-interest of the new business class. In parts of West Africa, however, a complicating factor exists which is independent of any of the forces described up to now. This is the introduction of European legal forms in advance of the circumstances that have elsewhere given rise to commercial transactions. The trading companies who in the early days established themselves on the coast obtained the land they needed by agreements concluded on equal terms with the local chiefs, and drawn up according to the forms of English law. At a rather later stage, courts of law were set up to which native cases were brought, and these courts assumed that land could be seized in payment of debt. Then Africans began to qualify as lawyers and to introduce into dealings between their fellow Africans the type of document, purporting to confer the type of right, appropriate to transfers of land under English law. Today in the Gold Coast it is the rule rather than the exception for cocoa farmers to base their claims to land on documents, many of which have actually no legal validity.[6]

A conclusion on the process of culture change in general, applicable over a wider field than that of land tenure, is that with the introduction of a money economy any position of economic privilege tends to become a source of personal gain. Such privileges are the right to allot land and the right to claim labour or tribute in kind. In the closed economy of the past, the personal advantages to be derived

[6] C. K. Meek, *op. cit.* p. 171.

51

from the exercise of such rights were limited and there was no tempta-
tion to the abuse of trust. Labour on the chief's fields produced a
communal reserve of food and provided maintenance for the retinue
which enabled him to carry out the tasks of government at the simple
level of those days; tribute in kind served the same purpose. The
chief could not use their entire yield for personal consumption, and
their concentration in his hands was part of a process of circulation
through the community; but as soon as they became convertible into
cash the position changed. The substitution for these obligations in
kind or in labour of payments to Native Administration treasuries
is the answer given to part of the problem; but where the right to
allot land, so fundamental an aspect of political authority in Africa,
is concerned, the way to prevent abuse without destroying authority
has not yet been found.

Another generalisation of wide application is that the conservative
force of tradition is never proof against the attraction of economic
advantage, provided that the advantage is sufficient and is clearly
recognised. In the case of land it is abundantly clear that the emotional
and religious attitudes towards it which are inculcated by native
tradition have not prevented the development of a commercial attitude.
The classic case of African conservatism—the reluctance of the stock-
owner to reduce the numbers of his stock and improve their quality—
is also explained in terms of the emotional and religious attitude towards
them that is so marked a feature of many African societies. But here
too it may be that the emphasis should be laid on inadequate incentive
rather than on conservatism as such. It is true also that the recognition
of economic opportunity does not spread at the same rate to all the
members of any society. In the case of land rights, changes designed
to affect the mass of the population meet with as much resistance as
de-stocking propaganda; the attempt to re-distribute oil-palm in
Nigeria so as to increase the efficiency of cultivation is a case in point.

Some observers see as the essence of developments of the type
described the emergence of the new system of values the acceptance
of which is necessary if African productivity is to be increased and
African standards of living raised. Others will regard them as
instances of what the late Godfrey Wilson termed 'uneven change'.[7] It
could certainly not be said that the stage at present reached represents
a satisfactory adjustment to new conditions.

[7] *The Analysis of Culture Change,* 1946.

VI

THE CONTRIBUTION OF
SOCIAL ANTHROPOLOGY TO THE STUDY OF
CHANGES IN AFRICAN LAND RIGHTS[1]

It has often been asserted that the absence of the conception of individual property in land is a retarding factor in the development of African agriculture. This proposition has more often been treated as an axiom than supported by arguments based on the observation of African systems in operation. I should like to examine its validity in the light of the studies that have been made by social anthropologists of (1) the actual nature of African systems of land rights and (2) the consequences which have followed the recognition or creation of individual property rights.

Of course I do not claim that all that I am going to say is esoteric knowledge which remained secret until social anthropologists penetrated its mysteries. Such a claim would be singularly inappropriate in this country, where Professor Guy Malengreau, whose special skill is, I think, that of a lawyer, has already most convincingly expounded several of the propositions that I am about to discuss.[2] I might, however, claim a certain common ground with him through the circumstances that the knowledge that we have of African institutions in the Congo has been very largely gathered by lawyers, who have done a part of the work that falls to anthropologists in British territories.

When Malinowski, at the time of the founding of the International African Institute in 1926, urged that the studies of anthropologists should be focused on those aspects of African society which were of significance for the framing of policy, he laid especial emphasis on systems of land rights as a subject of investigation. At that time African systems were widely misunderstood, and it is fair to say that the greater knowledge of their fundamental principles that we have today is due very largely to the stimulus given by him. Another British authority who has called attention to the importance of this question in Africa is Lord Hailey, who brought from his Indian experience the recognition that the type of land rights which are recognised or granted by the government can have a decisive influence on the development of an agricultural community. A panel of experts on land tenure convened at the Colonial Office in 1945, under his chairmanship, urged upon all African governments the need of a close study of the systems in operation in their territories and the changes which they were undergoing, as a basis for decisions as to the type of right which should now be recognised as valid. A good many such inquiries have been made, on lines which take the existing

[1] Paper read at a conference on changes in African land rights at the Institut Solvay, Brussels, January, 1956.
[2] Notably in his 'De l'accession des indigènes à la propriété foncière individuelle', *Zaire*, 1947, pp. 235-70, 399-434.

findings of social anthropology into account to a greater or lesser degree. But I should like to draw attention particularly to one or two intensive studies made by professional anthropologists.

The famous phrase of Arthur Young, 'the magic of property turns sand into gold', refers to a quite specific context—that of a system where individual property rights already exist, and are exercised by persons who hold them to the detriment of those who do not. It refers, in fact, to the insecurity of a tenant who has no protection against his landlord, and assumes an economy in which rights to the disposal of land are used as a source of commercial profit. There is no need to stress the fact that African traditional economies were not of this type. What then is the significance of the absence in African society of the conception of individual property in land?

The subject is sometimes discussed in terms of polar opposites—'individual' and 'communal' or 'collective' rights—and the assumption is made that any system must belong to one or other category. Analysis of the data obtained by anthropologists suggests rather that within any African system there are two types of right, which may be called rights of occupation and rights of administration, and that the latter are held by different persons in different societies.

Certain principles will be found to be of general application:

(1) Every person has the right to land for cultivation in virtue of his membership of some social group; (2) he has the right to remain in undisturbed occupation of this land and to transmit it to his heirs; (3) the group, or its representatives, have the right to veto any creation of rights in favour of non-members, and in certain cases to re-allocate land which has gone out of cultivation. Group rights come into being as a result of the principle that all a man's sons are his heirs; indeed, the land is often partitioned during the father's lifetime, as each son marries and a portion is allotted to his wife. Hence the group exercising joint rights is usually a group of kin. Sometimes, however, the overriding control is vested in a chief or headman whose authority extends over many others than his own kinsmen. In these cases the occupation of land depends upon political loyalty, and a landholder can be expelled as a punishment for disobedience. Here, and only here, can we speak of insecurity; and it is worth noting that it is not the insecurity of the tenant in relation to a landlord. The landlord, seeking to maximise his rent, readily exchanges one tenant for another. The chief seeks to maximise his following and does not readily drive away any subject; though we may agree that his decision that a subject is disloyal may sometimes be an arbitrary one.

If it is asserted that the absence of individual rights as we understand them is a deterrent to the adoption of commercial cultivation, we need only name a few export crops that have been taken up with enthusiasm by African farmers who did not possess these rights—cocoa in West Africa, coffee in Tanganyika, wattles and maize in Kenya. In the Congo, too, as M. Malengreau points out, the areas under coffee, cotton and groundnuts are steadily increasing.

54

Deduction from the logical possibilities of a situation does not always lead to the right conclusion as to what will happen. In one or two cases the rules of customary tenure are incompatible with forms of land use which might be commercially profitable. Suppose that the arable lands are by custom thrown open after the harvest for common grazing, as is the case in Basutoland. As long as this rule is respected no one can plant a permanent crop. But the history of change in African land systems is precisely the history of the manipulation of the traditional rules in order to profit by new opportunities, and, sooner or later, the rejection of those that are found to be too irksome. It can rarely be demonstrated that any customary restriction on individual enterprise has prevented the introduction of a new form of land use which offered a good hope of profit. It is on record from Basutoland that one chief prevented the planting of wheat, and even destroyed standing crops, because the growers claimed the wheat straw as their own property and so the right of communal grazing after harvest was restricted. Yet it is taken for granted in Basutoland today that one of every man's three fields is planted with wheat.[3] It is a matter for investigation how far the assertion often ascribed to African farmers, that they are afraid to have good fields because 'the chief will be jealous' or 'their neighbours will be jealous', is a genuine reason, and how far it is an excuse; and the same comment applies to the statement that people are afraid to excel their neighbours for fear of witchcraft. Witchcraft inspired by envy may be invoked as the explanation of some actual disaster, but it does not follow that anyone shuns prosperity in order to avoid the risk of witchcraft. It is significant that this kind of explanation of reluctance to improve methods of cultivation is most often heard in the regions where it has been hard to find a profitable crop. It is the answer to propaganda for soil conservation measures or for measures to improve the yield of the traditional food crops, from which the African farmer rarely expects to get benefits commensurate with the extra work involved.

In the process of manipulation of the traditional system in response to the opportunity of making profit from rights in land, the sphere of independent action by the small group or the individual right-holder is steadily increasing at the expense of that of control by the representatives of the wider collectivity. Although offers by governments to confer documentary title on anyone applying for it have rarely met with much response, persons who see the opportunity to dispose profitably of rights in land are eager to do so without appealing to any group authority. Commonly, too, the extent of the group whose members are willing to allow the re-allocation of surplus lands tends to grow narrower; as land becomes scarce, those in possession become more and more unwilling to relinquish control of fields which they may need for their sons, and if it has acquired a commercial value they want to enjoy the advantage from this. Developments among

[3] H. Ashton, *The Basuto*, 1952, pp. 146 and 148.

55

the Kikuyu, for example, illustrate this process. Of course it is logically possible that the problem of shortage could be solved by the insistence of those in authority on their right to re-distribute the fields, and this is the solution we find in Basutoland. In this respect the Basuto seem to be peculiar. Why? Anthropologists have not sought to answer this question by comparative study, but I would suggest two reasons. The first is that among them land is not held by kin groups, but allocated to individuals by the political heads of districts, so that there is no close knot of kinsmen anxious to preserve the land for their descendants; and the second that, despite the scarcity of land, it has not acquired a commercial value sufficient to tempt the Basuto to make independent arrangements for the disposal of fields which are surplus to their needs or more than their man-power can plough. This latter reason must be associated with the fact that there is in any case a better income to be made from work outside Basutoland than from the produce of the land.

The farmer who has no security in Africa today is not the holder of land as member of a group, but he who has acquired his land by a cash transaction and does not know whether his claim is to be regarded as valid. Will the courts of the area hold that outright sale is now permitted under customary law? Will the sale be ruled invalid because all the members of the right-holding group were not consulted? Will the seller try to regain the land as soon as it has been planted up with cocoa or coffee, claiming that under customary law land pledged to an outsider can be redeemed at any time? It is for persons in this position, a position which has come into existence only in response to the new commercial opportunities, that there is need for individual title.

What happens in those cases where individual title has in fact been granted? There are a few cases in the African territories of the Commonwealth where the lands of a whole social unit have been parcelled out in holdings as individual property, held under European and not tribal law. The best known are the districts of the Transkei, in the Union of South Africa, which were surveyed under the Glen Grey Act of 1894, and the so-called *mailo* lands which were allotted in freehold to a thousand Ganda chiefs by the Uganda Agreement of 1900. Outside the Transkeian districts there are some villages in the Cape where land has been allotted to groups of Africans on individual title, or where it was actually purchased by the ancestors of the present inhabitants. In the Keiskammahoek District a sociological survey made a few years ago compared the present situation in villages where land was held on 'communal' and on individual tenure;[4] and for Buganda a study has recently been made by an African anthropologist, Mr. A. B. Mukwaya.[5]

[4] M. E. Elton Mills and M. Wilson, *Land Tenure*, Keiskammahoek Rural Survey, vol. iv, 1952.
[5] A. B. Mukwaya, *Land Tenure in Buganda*, East African Institute of Social Research, 1953.

Since I took Arthur Young's saying for my opening text, I might introduce a summary of their observations by asking how the 'magic of property' has actually worked. Has either Keiskammahoek or Buganda been turned by it from sand into gold? Alas, we all know that in general the soil of Africa is changing in the opposite direction. I have suggested already that the incentive to demand the unrestricted control of land is the short-term profit to be made by disposing of it and not the long-term advantage of wise investment in it.

To the question, what does a tropical farmer do when given the full control of his land? the history of India has supplied an answer. He uses it as security for credit, but the money he raises is rarely invested in the land. This difficulty, and the dilemma that unless he can use his land in this way he cannot raise capital for productive purposes, are much debated. I know of no actual investigation by an anthropologist of such a situation, but I imagine that, if he were asked to comment upon it, he would look outside the narrow field of land rights at the whole system of values of the society. Is it necessary for a man to make displays on social and ceremonial occasions in order to gain esteem? Is it difficult for many men to attain the standard they aim at within the limits of their income? Do many of them really believe that long-term investment will in the end be worth while? Have they even ever been told that it will, in terms that they appreciate?

In the studies that I have mentioned, however, it is more interesting to see how far conceptions of the mutual obligations of kinsmen, and of other traditional social relationships, have modified a system of land rights which so many Europeans see as the key to African advancement, the way of escape from meaningless restrictions on the enterprise of an intelligent man.

The Keiskammahoek survey was carried out on lines first suggested by Malinowski; the history of a number of plots was traced out in detail, showing how they had been transmitted, subdivided and so on. When this method of study was first suggested some thirty years ago, the comment was made that it would take 'an anthropological Methuselah' to complete the necessary inquiries. The value of properly selected samples, however, is now recognised, and in 1951 an article in the *Journal of African Administration*, which is published by the U.K. Colonial Office for the information of officials serving in the African territories, recommended just this method to anyone proposing to make a land tenure survey.

In the village held under 'communal tenure', as the South African authorities call it, ten families were originally allotted holdings, but up to twenty years ago persons other than their descendants were sometimes given land. As is traditional with the south-eastern Bantu, the allocation of new fields was made by the headman. Now it is in practice the responsibility of the Native Commissioner, and the principles of customary tenure are being interpreted in a manner consistent with the aims of government policy. Of these the most important is that of providing land for cultivation to everyone who has a claim in virtue of village membership. This is in line with traditional principles, but now that land is scarce, it appears that another principle of the traditional system has greater weight with the African villagers, namely, the unbroken association of the holder and his heirs with any plot of land once allocated. In order not to lose this interest in his holding, a man who goes away to work will 'lend' it to a kinsman, and to prevent a field being transferred outside his family when he dies, a man may give one to his son during his lifetime. Thus we see again that individual interests assert themselves within the framework of a 'communal' system as soon as there is any competition for land. Men with no land, of course, invoke the 'communal' principle of redistribution.

Where land has been purchased, no control can be exercised over its disposal. In a village founded in this way, holdings had at one time been mortgaged or sold, but the practice had ceased as people became alive to the danger of losing their land.

It is often assumed that, once individual title has been granted, the land in question will continue to be the property of a single person. The history of Keiskammahoek shows that this is not the case. In fact, the holders behave as far as possible as they would if they had acquired their land in the traditional way by allocation from the chief or, as happens in other parts of Africa, simply by being the first to clear the bush. As long as there is surplus land available, the essentials of the process are the same.

Sometimes, when a holding is marked out, it is intentionally made larger than the area that one household can cultivate on the assumption that the surplus will be available for the next generation. If the original holding allows no surplus, or if there is no demarcation of boundaries, then the ideal is for one son to remain on his father's land while the others push out into the surrounding bush. This process has been well described for the Kamba of Kenya by Mr. D. W. Penwill. The tradition he records is of a time when the tribe were penetrating into new country and were ready to abandon fields they had made for virgin land farther ahead; in that case land already cleared would be handed over for some kind of consideration, but a kinsman had the first right to acquire it. In the freehold village at Keiskammahoek the only way of expansion was to buy more land; but as long as the law allowed this, all Africans who could did so, and the holding originally purchased went to only one son of the buyer. But where this expansion was not possible the land was divided among all the sons, since it would be wrong for one to 'eat the inheritance alone' and leave his brothers landless. Sometimes the lot is not divided and so group rights come into being; sometimes boundaries are formally marked out in the presence of all villagers. In either case the principle which has priority is the claim of kinship. Eventually, of course, the point is reached where further sub-division is considered impracticable even by African standards; then some men must become landless. In only one respect are the legal implications of freehold acted upon. Since rights cannot be forfeited by absence, some land-owners live and work in urban areas, and some of these lease their land for rent; if they have a kinsman in the village, they will let him work the land without charge.

Thus, freehold gives security, but secure tenure does not lead to the improvement of the land. 'Communal tenure' does not give security, but this is because the right of administration is now in the hands of a European whose ideas as to what constitutes a claim to land are not those of African tradition. The Native Commissioner recognises the claims of close kinsmen to inherit land, but would prefer to a distant kinsman, or a minor, some man who has been long in the village without receiving an allotment. Thus the claim to land as a member of a kin-group, the basis of the traditional system, is no longer secure. In fact the extent of the group within which re-allocation is allowed has been widened by European action.

An obvious point on which I have not yet touched, which was not obvious to Arthur Young, is that the units of land held by Africans under either of these systems are too small for any holder to derive an adequate income from farming alone. The confident assertion, 'Give a man the secure possession of a bleak rock and he will turn it into a garden', was conceived in the era when new technical discoveries seemed to offer unlimited hopes of improvement, and before agronomists had begun to wrestle with the difficulties of tropical soils and climates.

In Buganda the story is different. Here, as is well known, the Uganda Agreement allotted a total area of 8000 square miles in free-hold to persons described as 'chiefs or private landowners', believed already to have the rights which freehold title would merely confirm. Here there was no question of holdings of uneconomic size. Since the number of persons entitled to freehold was estimated at a thousand, the average area of an estate should have been eight square miles. In fact the whole area was not allotted, and the number of claimants was nearly 4000, so that the grants actually made were of smaller area. On the other hand, very much larger estates were allotted to the Kabaka, his close relatives and his principal chiefs.

Here one can certainly see how the landlords turned to profit the new rights with which they found themselves endowed. But it is even more interesting to observe the persistence of the traditional pattern of relationships between the holder of administrative rights and the cultivator of the land. The ways in which the system has developed have been analysed by Mr. A. B. Mukwaya, on the basis of study of the central land register of Buganda and of the detailed history of 98 estates in two selected areas.

The total number of owners of freehold land has increased to a figure which Mr. Mukwaya estimates at between 45,000 and 55,000. Hence the original grantees must have disposed of a good deal of their land. They did so in many ways. Some made gifts of portions to kinsmen or followers whom they wished to keep near them, but in many more cases a part of the original estate was sold. Indeed the sales of land began when the owners had to pay the fees for survey. Other sales have been made 'for such purposes as the purchase of motor-cars, the building of houses, or to raise capital to start shops or commercial companies and even to pay for luxurious living'.[6] Land is also sold to pay for the education of boys who then follow other callings than that of the farmer.

Why is it bought? Sometimes as a form of investment, but often because of the higher status accorded to the landowner as against the tenant. An essential of this status is that the landowner has his own tenants, who are subject to his authority in a relationship analogous to the traditional one between chief and subject. Hence not many men buy land to farm by their own or hired labour. The desire for security plays its part, but security is not sought in order to put capital into the land.

The claim of brothers to share an inheritance is still recognised in Buganda, but here group rights do not develop because the separate shares are demarcated, and because the unrestricted right of each heir to dispose of his land is recognised. In the cases recorded in detail the principal heir took by far the larger share of the original estate, but all the heirs gave away and sold portions of their land, with the result of creating a large number of small units (under 20 acres).

Indeed it is abundantly proven that the magic of property operates only in a very specific context, and no modern plans for the improvement of African agriculture rely on this principle alone. On the contrary, the greatest importance is now attached by some colonial governments to the retention of such control as may enable them to regulate farming methods. This itself is a source of difficulty in places where African farmers see that other Africans, or Europeans, have rights more extensive than they are themselves being offered; or where Africans trained in the principles of European law appeal to it as representing a system enjoyed by Europeans but denied by them to Africans. The political arguments for the grant of individual property rights may well be decisive in the end, but an anthropologist would suggest that they must be distinguished from attempts to advocate it as a contribution to the productivity of agriculture.

The Ganda landlords readily recognised the opportunity of deriving revenue from their tenants, the more so as the payments that they claimed were analogous with the tribute formerly due to the chief. The Uganda Government induced the African Government of Buganda to pass legislation fixing the sums to be paid by the tenant and protecting him from arbitrary eviction. The aims of this measure are beyond criticism. But one of its effects is that landlords who wish to lay out their land for mechanised cultivation are unable to find areas of suitable size on which there are no tenant holdings.

These facts abundantly demonstrate that proprietary rights in

[6] *Op. cit.*, p. 35.

themselves have but little magical effect. Up to a point, they are not a prerequisite of development. M. Malengreau has argued that the traditional systems, in which rights in land depend directly upon cultivation, give a greater incentive to production than one in which a proprietor can leave his land undeveloped without losing his right to it. He points out too that the direct incentive of a good price is sufficient to encourage the planting of cash crops. In fact there has rarely been any difficulty in inducing Africans to plant cash crops. The problem which concerns agronomists is the indifference of most Africans to those improvements in technique which are essential if the yield and quality of crops is to be increased or even maintained. This indifference is general: it cannot be said to be significantly greater in the case of those farmers who hold their land on some form of lease from right-holders, or who have bought it in an area where it is doubtful whether the sale will be regarded as valid. Nor can it be held to depend directly on the fact that land cannot be offered as security for credit. A social anthropologist would look for reasons in a wider field: in the whole range of traditional ideas about agriculture, in the tendency to find supernatural explanations for such misfortunes as the failure of crops, in experience of cases where the advice of the agricultural department proved unsound, in that preference for short-term, clearly envisaged benefits over more remote ones which is certainly not peculiar to Africans.

He would note that the actual work of cultivation is done mostly by women, who have far less contact with Europeans than do men, and are therefore least prepared to understand their exhortations and most disposed to regard these as mere tiresome interference by the authorities. He would also ask what is the constitution of the working team at the peak periods of farming activities. We know already that at these times no single household has enough man-power to complete these operations by itself. Many peoples have the system whereby all villagers work on each farm in turn, and are rewarded by beer at the end of the day. With others, every young man who is betrothed brings his age-mates to work on the field of his future father-in-law. Where cash incomes are high enough, wage-labour is employed. But until this point has been reached, the question what additional labour is needed, and where it can be found, is relevant to all recommendations for technical improvement.

In certain parts of Africa the anthropologist would observe a sense of insecurity that has quite a different source—the belief that Europeans are advocating the improvement of the land simply in order to take possession of it when the Africans have done the work, and, as the corollary of this fear and resentment, the conviction that there is no technical problem that the return of alienated lands to Africans would not solve.

The essential contribution of the social anthropologist to this subject is that he is trained to see any single change, of the kind that can be effected by legislation, against the background of an existing system of

61

relationships and an existing standard of values. The new rules will be manipulated by the persons to whom they are applied in accordance with the views they hold of their own advantage. Some will seek to derive economic profit from the new situation, possibly in other ways than those the legislator hoped to encourage. Some will seek to realise old values, such as the close contiguity and co-operation of kinsfolk (which, as M. Malengreau points out, we praise when its consequences suit us), or the prestige of a landholding chief with followers grouped round him. What will happen in a given case depends on the relative strength of different social pressures and cannot be predicted in detail; but studies by social anthropologists have done a good deal to indicate the kind of development that may be expected.

VII

SELF-GOVERNMENT OR GOOD GOVERNMENT?

One of the most remarkable features of the last few years has been the change in the relations between colonial territories and the metropolitan powers responsible for their government. In some cases these changes have been brought about by force, where peoples who had been subject to Japanese occupation seized the opportunity created by the interregnum after the Japanese surrender to establish their own governments claiming to be recognised as independent. This occurred in Indo-China and in the Netherlands Indies. In Indo-China the demands of the local leaders went far beyond anything that had been contemplated in France before the war, though in 1945 the French Provisional Government had announced its intention to establish a federal relationship with Indo-China, itself already nominally a 'federation' of colonies and protectorates. The Dutch on the other hand had been contemplating proposals for fuller self-government for the Indies before the war, but none of the plans envisaged then gave the degree of independence claimed by the Indonesian Republic. In both these territories the metropolitan power has found it necessary to use armed force to assert a position which it is not prepared to give up; in both cases it is uncertain whether the former rulers may not have to surrender even what seems to them to be the essential minimum of control.

In India there was no armed conflict. The aim of ultimate independence had long been accepted in Britain, and differences of opinion turned on the question whether the time was ripe. Yet, when the decision to withdraw was finally taken, perhaps the determining consideration was that the British position in India could not be maintained without the use of armed force on a scale greater than was held to be morally justifiable. The situation was similar in Burma.

Yet the history of recent years is not simply a history of reluctant concession to force. The feeling that the rule of any people by a government alien to it and not responsible to it is very hard to justify, and indeed can only be justified in so far as it prepares for its own extinction, is coming to be more and more widely held; and that not only among the subjects of this rule and the peoples of nations which, having themselves few or no overseas territories, are quicker to see the defects of 'imperialism' than to regard it as a historical necessity, but by public opinion in the nations which have colonies. The response to this feeling in British colonial policy has been an overhaul of the constitution of all the colonies and their modification so as greatly to increase the weight given to representatives of local opinion. Ceylon now has full Dominion status. Malta has responsible government in internal affairs. The legislature with a majority of unofficial members is now the rule rather than the exception, in contrast to the system that was general before the war, under which a majority of the members were official, and measures could be carried at any time by the votes of the official bloc. With the unofficial majority a Government Bill can be defeated on the floor of the House. Since this system is still short of full responsible government, and the executive is not removable by an adverse vote in the legislature, the Governor still retains power, through the right of certification, to enact measures deemed essential. Though some colonial nationalists interpret this provision as nullifying the rights conceded to them, it is recognised that the power of certification exists only for exceptional cases of absolute necessity. In general, unofficial representation has been increased and included in Executive as well as Legislative Councils, and the franchise has been extended. The two major West African colonies now have unofficial African majorities, and in East and Central Africa there are, or will be shortly, African members in all the Legislative Councils.

The process that has been set on foot must go on with increasing momentum. There are enough historical examples to show that the intermediate stages on the way to self-government are regarded by the peoples concerned always as something more than positions to be consolidated, always as springboards for the next advance.

What are the consequences likely to be, for the world and for the peoples most directly concerned? Can one draw up a balance sheet of advantages and disadvantages? Or is the process one of pure advantage, an instance of that 'progress' in which our grandparents had so much more confidence than we have?

We have all asserted, over and over again, that good government is no substitute for self-government, and where we ourselves are concerned we have no doubt that it is true. Hence the uneasiness of our conscience towards the colonial peoples subject to our rule. Have we then found here an absolute in the field of politics—a principle that holds good without qualifications in any time or place? If so, why should not all the imperial powers withdraw at once from their dependencies? The most insistent of their critics have not asked for this, though in the case of the Far Eastern colonies America would not allow her troops to take part in the re-establishment of the colonial governments. In Africa ten-year time-limits have sometimes been mentioned.

This suggests qualifications of the principle. Are there circumstances in which independence would not be an improvement on colonial rule? Some colonial nationalists would retort with an appeal to the absolute; material conditions may in some ways deteriorate, but this is of no account in comparison with the value of freedom itself. Others would assert that if in some respects—notably the level of material resources and social services—colonial territories are at a lower level than the independent nations, this is actually a result of their colonial status, and emancipation is the remedy.

There is one wholly logical position, if one has the courage to accept it. It is the one summed up in the statement that 'Everyone has the right to be miserable in his own way'. If a people prefer autocracy to democracy, arbitrary justice to the rule of law, contaminated water to drains, poverty with leisure to hard work and higher real incomes, it is no one else's business. From this position one can look on at communal massacres, dacoity, famine or near famine, and reflect that whatever sufferings these events may cause to however many individuals, they are as nothing to the recognition of the principle that every people has the right to conduct its own affairs in its own way. One may regret these events, but one has no right to invoke the argument that under colonial rule they would not have occurred; and, indeed, one is obliged to admit that independent States have allowed or caused equally great sufferings to as many or more individuals among their own subjects and those of their neighbours. One must set against them, too, that sense of a new dignity, of an advance in human status, that observers tell us is apparent in the very bearing of the ordinary man in those countries which have recently won independence.

But is this the whole story? Is there nothing but complacency and hypocrisy—self-deception and the deception of others—in the belief that colonial rule brought some amelioration to the conditions of its subjects? Was the reluctance of some sections of opinion in Britain to see that happening in India which has happened a mere cloak for economic and military interest?

Undoubtedly the conception of 'the white man's burden' has been invoked to give a colour of public-spirited self-sacrifice to many activities undertaken out of sheer self-interest. The argument that it is a moral duty to make two blades of grass grow where one grew before is the basis even today of the claim that the European *entrepreneur* in the colonies has a moral right to conditions in which he can make a profit. While it is true that few colonial enterprises have yielded large profits, that is a very different thing from saying that they were undertaken solely in a spirit of service to humanity. It would be more honest to admit that the commercial motive in the acquisition and retention of colonies has always been self-interested—which is not the same as to say anti-social—whether or not the colonies have gained by its working out.

Without accepting the crude theory that colonial peoples as a whole have been 'exploited' for the benefit of the metropolitan powers, one can see certain respects in which it is quite clear that the colonies have been at a disadvantage through the fact that trade policy is not determined locally and that control of the most important business enterprise is outside the colony. Tariff policies are decided by the metropolitan powers primarily in their own interests. This will be less easy in the case of colonial legislatures with an unofficial majority, unless these questions are considered important enough to necessitate the use of the Governor's power of certification. The business firms, with whom alone members of the local population could have learnt the techniques of management, have given very little opportunity to such young men. They are often able to establish a monopoly of import trade and control retail prices. They have shown little benevolence towards the development of local industries which might compete with their imports, if they have not actively opposed it. In an age where it is accepted that a share of the profits of enterprise is taken by the State for expenditure in the general interests of the community, far too large a part of this share has been taken by the treasuries of the metropolitan powers.

And yet they have introduced capital into the colonies, and increased their productivity, and with it their national income and the resources, small as they have been, available for the provision of social services.

So we return to the question whether, for the colonial peoples, the right to be miserable in their own way involves their continuance at the standard of life which had been attained in the days of subsistence or barter economy. The appeal to this right is valid against those who liked to believe they were performing a noble action in teaching lazy peoples the dignity of labour. Today there are still some people in many colonies whose lives have changed little in the past sixty years and who are not interested in what we should consider improvement. But colonial nationalism is not the assertion of *their* point of view. On the contrary, their existence is one of the counts in the indictment of the colonial ruler by the colonial nationalists. It proves, they say, the hollowness of such metaphors as 'trusteeship' or even 'partnership'. Advancement, progress, is their aim, that progress which, they argue, has been denied them up till now.

The progress sought is in material standards—better social services, higher individual incomes. It depends therefore on an increasing national income, and this depends on higher productivity, and this in turn on the provision of capital. The capital must come from outside because the margin of resources available within the colonies is not sufficient to supply what would be necessary for a really substantial increase in productivity. In the British colonies it has been provided on a very limited scale since 1940 from the Colonial Development and Welfare Vote, and the Overseas Development Corporation created in 1947 is intended to supply it on a much larger scale for purely economic purposes. Although these arrangements involve no element of profit for the private investor, they are yet regarded with a certain suspicion by colonial nationalists, who see in them a perpetuation of external control.

Here we come to the real dilemma. Colonial leaders desire something which it is entirely impossible that they should produce for themselves. While their people remain in their dependent position, the metropolitan powers may provide this—not from altruism but from mixed motives: the recognition that eventual independence is inevitable and will be meaningless if it has not a sound economic foundation, the desire to increase the total of world trade, an urgent demand in the metropolitan country for a particular commodity.

France followed Britain in announcing the creation of a colonial development fund, though the instability of French finances since that was done has perhaps stultified that measure.

When the present colonies are free, however, there will be only two alternatives. Either they will by that time have attained a level of productivity at which capital for further development can be supplied from local saving—which does not seem very likely—or they will have to obtain it from abroad on ordinary commercial terms. For those colonies which have already become independent only the second alternative is available. It has been approached in various ways. The Philippines—not without strong local opposition—have accorded special privileges to United States capital. The Indonesian Republic at one time expressed its readiness to welcome the return of Dutch enterprise to Java. In Burma foreign capital is to be expropriated.

The most likely general prognostic seems to be a policy of economic nationalism, in the sense of heavy taxation of foreign firms and the imposition of various restrictive conditions on them—a policy which is not calculated to attract new capital. A distinguished West Indian economist has expressed the view that, in the absence of sufficient judgment to hit the perfect mean, it is better to accept the investment of capital on terms which will attract it—'exploitation' if you like—than to impose restrictions which can only act as a deterrent to investors. But it does not seem likely that many people in the colonies will listen to him.

Capital is indispensable to the aims of the colonial nationalists. A factor about which one cannot speak with the same certainty is efficiency. Efficiency, precision, surgical asepsis, the nut fitting the bolt, the airman making his rendezvous at the scheduled time to the exact second, characterise a mechanical civilisation based on the application of the principles of science. In the sphere of production, efficiency involves attention to quality and to output per man-hour; in that of administration, impersonal decisions, perseverance in overcoming obstacles, a railway time-table on which the traveller can rely. To achieve it requires a considerable output of mental and physical energy. To certain classes in certain nations it is a fetish, to other sections of humanity a ridiculous fad.

The removal from key posts in colonial territories of a large number of persons who worship efficiency will have its effect on the way things are done in future in those territories. Will the result of their going be felt in the form of hardship? In a great many cases, probably not. If trains are not clean or punctual, surgical instruments not always sterilised, university qualifications not recognised as equivalent to those obtainable in Britain, this is a small price to pay for freedom and it may not even be felt as a price. But a point can come where the price of a decline in efficiency is generally felt even if the cause is not recognised. For one thing which ultimately depends upon efficiency is the level of incomes. Now, however much colonial peoples may question the other benefits which their rulers claim to have conferred upon them, they do not question the desirability of a money income; and if productive efficiency should decline to a point where incomes fall appreciably from even their present low level, this will be very widely felt as a hardship.

At the moment, in the newly-emancipated countries, production has very seriously declined. The major reason is not a decline in efficiency but sheer physical insecurity. The Viet-Namese and Indonesians can put the responsibility for this on the refusal of their former rulers to abdicate their position, but the Indians and Burmans cannot.

This brings one to the final question in debate: how far has emancipation resulted in—to put it as euphemistically as possible—a decrease in personal security, and how far is this to be regarded as a part of every man's right to be miserable in his own way? It is difficult to take up a position on this question which cannot be criticised as hypocritical. Who are we, who have reduced the cities of Western Germany to rubble, to hold up our hands in horror at communal massacres in India? The answer is, I think, that it is not a question of comparing the magnitude of crimes. All destruction, all slaughter, are deplorable, and any island, however small, in which destruction and slaughter are prevented is so much to the good. India, up to August, 1947, was such an island, and a large one—a single State possessing authority sufficient to prevent slaughter on a large scale. Now the Indian sub-continent is divided between two major States (with a number of minor ones) in extremely strained relations and not apparently possessing this authority. This is a net loss to the world, and it is hard to see who gains by it in India.

This Indian problem has its analogues elsewhere—the problem of a territory on which unity has been imposed by external force, where the inhabitants are united in the desire for independence but divided by interests just as strong, where the question 'Independence for whom?' is at the back of the constitutional demands of today in which each party is seeking to stake its claim for tomorrow. Outside India the problems of a plural society have been created by immigration fostered by the metropolitan powers, of Dutch in Indonesia, Chinese in Malaya, Jews in Palestine, Europeans and Indians in East Africa. In each case the immigrants have had an economic equipment superior to that of the indigenous people and have established themselves at a higher economic level. In each case the ruling power, after favouring the immigration, has felt itself bound to protect the interests of the indigenous population as the weaker party. In each case, with the exception of Indonesia, it has been driven to modify this policy under pressure from the immigrants. Disunity in Indonesia appears to be a matter of local rather than communal interests. In all the other cases communal claims are being pressed, and such voices as may be raised in favour of co-operation are barely heard. Even where there are no rivalries between communities, the question may arise whether the nationalists do represent a nation or merely a group drawn largely from a limited area in the colony for which they speak.

We cannot tell when, in each separate case, the moment will come for that transfer of power which is now recognised as both inevitable and logically necessary. We only know that it is much nearer than anyone would have dreamed ten years ago, and that whatever may by that time have been done to prepare for it will be short of the ideal aimed at by those—and they do exist—who seek to make colonial rule a means to the advancement of colonial peoples.

The task now is to lay such foundations as will give the colonies the best possible start when the time for transfer comes. On the economic side this involves a development policy which will result in a permanent increase in productivity, and this in turn involves the active interest of the people whose hands are going to do the work in putting the policy into effect. It involves the securing of goodwill, and it involves the training of many more persons both in manual skills and in the tasks of supervision and management. In all these directions the problem is to make up for the time lost during the era when paternalistic efficiency was the method and the justification of colonial rule. Nobody is to blame for not having foreseen the change in the climate of ideas; but many will be blamed in the not so distant future if the necessary adjustments to it are not made. Not the least of the difficulties to be overcome will be the conservatism of the individuals whose co-operation is sought—mistrust of new methods perhaps complicated by mistrust of those who advocate them. Any development which requires the individual action of millions of people entails endless patient persuasion—if the method of force is rejected.

On the political side, it is hoped that the co-operation of the leaders of local opinion in constructive plans will be more readily offered now that the weight accorded to them in the political organisation has been increased. Yet it would be an illusion to imagine that this co-operation will be secured without unremitting tact and sympathy and much patience. Above all this patience will be needed in the colonies where there are communal divisions. We have seen the tragic consequences of letting these take their course. There may be circumstances where such divisions are irreconcilable, but where there is any hope of finding common ground it must surely be a major task of the governing power to try to bring the two sides together.

It is not sufficient to rejoice in the approach of the day of freedom; it is essential to realise how immense a task has to be done, and in how little time, to secure that the price of freedom shall not be too high.

VIII

ANTHROPOLOGY AND THE UNDER-DEVELOPED TERRITORIES[1]

In these days every student of a specialised subject is liable to be challenged to demonstrate the value of his study. It is not enough to say that knowledge is good because it is knowledge. Different branches of knowledge are competing for students' time, and, even more anxiously, for money to pay for research. In the social sciences, where we concentrate on the various aspects of human behaviour, we scholars on our side are apt to think that if only people in authority would listen to us, they might take more intelligent decisions and make fewer mistakes.

In the presence of this audience there is no need to define the scope of social anthropology, nor to emphasise the aspects of policy to which knowledge of it is relevant. I think your great scholar, Dr. Snouck Hurgronje, was ahead of anyone in the English-speaking world in realising that the traditional customs of colonial peoples are not just a matter of antiquarian interest, that they do not simply vanish when confronted with what we call civilisation, and that Europeans who are responsible for the government of these peoples must understand the rules and values by which they live.

It seems to have been only at the beginning of this century that American and English writers first urged that Governments should take anthropological knowledge into account. In America the occasion was the war with Spain, which resulted in America acquiring what any other nation would have called colonies. The American sociologist Keller published an article in the *Yale Review* in 1903, which seems oddly naive when one reads it today. In his mind all the time is the simple notion of the survival of the fittest. Modern industrial civilisation is clearly the fittest. In competition with its bearers, the indigenous inhabitants of various colonial areas have become extinct, or nearly so, and the rest must either adopt it or become extinct in their turn. But if we understand the indigenous cultures, we can make the process as painless as possible. 'Contending human races should be able to ease, at least, the extinction of their heavily handicapped antagonists.' That was Keller's view.

In Britain, anthropologists first tried to get a hearing in the South African War, after we had annexed the Transvaal and Orange Free State. They had had plenty of time to learn that the Bantu population there were not going to become extinct. In the context of the discussions of those days, they thought it necessary to point this out. They begged Mr. Joseph Chamberlain to appoint a commission to study the customs and institutions of these populations before any

[1] Text of a lecture given to the Netherlands Africa Institute and the Royal Institute for the Indies at Amsterdam, 30th October, 1950.

70

legislation affecting them was passed. After many delays Mr. Chamberlain replied that 'the officials of the new colonies are most fully occupied in the task of organising the administration and in dealing with the numerous questions of pressing political importance which arise'. As a matter of fact, soon after the close of the war a commission was appointed to lay down principles of native policy, but it did not include any anthropologists.

Of course Keller took too simple a view when he thought the non-European peoples were doomed to extinction. But it does seem to be true that their cultures are fated to lose many of their most distinctive features. The colonial powers have brought their subjects within the orbit of western civilisation. They have taught them to work for wages, and have taught some of them to read and write, and to aspire to professions that belong to the civilisation of the western world. Today the indigenous peoples themselves want to adopt western civilisation—or rather, some of them want some features of it. The conflicts and difficulties that we see among them today arise out of the fact that their adaptation is incomplete, and that fact itself is due to the contrast between their values and systems of obligation, their methods of social co-operation, and our own. We may not be as sure as Keller was that we know how to resolve these conflicts, but certainly there is only one person qualified to analyse them, and he is the anthropologist.

Anthropologists have always demanded a sympathetic hearing for the point of view of the peoples they study. One of the paradoxes of the colonial situation is that, apart from anthropologists and some administrators, most of the individuals who have direct dealings with indigenous peoples, and claim to 'know the native', see them through a mist of hostile prejudice—the irritation that arises out of misunderstanding, and the prejudice that every unthinking person has against people whose ways are different from his own. The modern anthropologist has to live in daily contact with the people he is studying, speak their language, and understand how *they* look on the new world that governments and employers have created. They become his friends, and unless he is an unusually diplomatic person, he often finds himself constrained to defend them against the kind of ill-informed criticism that he meets when he comes back to European circles. More important, his theory of society tells him that every society has its own inherent logic. It makes sense for the people who live in it. However barbarous its institutions may seem to Europeans, the native people can defend them—and not merely by saying, 'It is our custom'. The anthropologist can see objective reasons why practices that we condemn provide answers for the problems of the societies where we find them. They are crude answers, no doubt, but there are few indigenous institutions that could be dismissed as sheer barbarity or sheer stupidity, and simply destroyed, without leaving a gap that has to be filled. Because he knows this, the anthropologist is supposed to be a reactionary—a person who looks on the past as the ideal, who sees outmoded customs in a romantic light and stands in the way of progress. This criticism sometimes comes from the educated, nationalist, groups in the colonies, and sometimes from the anthropologist's own compatriots. At the present time most thinking people are convinced that there must be a very rapid adaptation in indigenous societies if they are to meet the problems of the modern world. This is as true of countries like Burma and Indonesia, which are now autonomous, as it is of territories still under colonial rule. I think there is actually no anthropologist who is not aware of this fact, though there are some who say it does not concern them—that they are interested in the simpler human societies simply as objects of study.

Why then should anthropologists, who claim to have penetrated more deeply than others into colonial societies, and who also claim to be the champions of the people whose lives we study—why should we have misgivings about the changes which are taking place among them? I think we could make a number of answers.

One is that our analysis shows how complex the problems are. We are not faced with a simple question of speeding up the rate of change, but rather with what Godfrey Wilson, a brilliant young British anthropologist who died during the war, called a situation of 'uneven change'. Social change follows the line of least resistance. People are readily induced to adopt new ways by the prospect of immediate gain. They readily throw off old-fashioned restraints if the new world offers them an escape from such restraints. They are not so ready to accept new types of obligation appropriate to the new types of economic relationship.

The layman interprets this situation in terms of the character of the peoples concerned—they are lazy, they are dishonest, they are self-seeking. The anthropologist knows that people's values are not born in them but come to them from example and teaching and experience, so he seeks the explanation elsewhere. To him the society we should like to see is not just an agglomeration of individuals who show the qualities of character that we like to think belong to western civilisation, but an integrated society. By an integrated society he means one in which established institutions, and the rights, obligations and values associated with them, are generally accepted. To its members a society of this kind is an intelligible world in which their place is clear. The peasant societies of the tropical regions were of this type before they were brought into the orbit of the world market. Their material standards were very low, they had not the security of life and limb that western rule gave them, the opportunities of advancement open to individuals were limited, but they were integrated wholes. Some anthropologists have attached so much value to this fact that they have argued that it compensates for all the limitations of life in such a society in comparison with our own. Others, though they have not gone so far, have insisted on the difficulties of re-organising society in a period of rapid change, and have urged that, in so far as western governments can control the rate of change, they should do so, and should at least not destroy indigenous institutions which still retain their vitality. This was one of the arguments used in support of the British policy of Indirect Rule, and I think equally of the Dutch respect for indigenous authorities in Indonesia. Of course the policy itself did not depend on the advocacy of anthropologists. In so far as it was not imposed by necessity, it was the result of a spirit of tolerance which men like Lugard did not have to learn from anthropologists. Today the more popular view is that all indigenous institutions must disappear as soon as possible. The colonial peoples must transform themselves as soon as possible into modern states with all the institutions of the west. And if they are to have, and maintain, the independence that all are demanding and some have secured, they certainly must do this on the political side. In the British territories the most remarkable instance of such transformation that can be observed at the moment is the new constitution of the Gold Coast, which is to come into force in 1951. A Legislative Assembly is to be elected by universal suffrage, and from it will be formed an Executive Council whose members will have ministerial status. This council will differ from a Cabinet only in that it will be responsible to the Governor and not the Legislature. This will be a most interesting experiment.

The fact that British policy is now set on these lines has been quoted as an argument that anthropology is now obsolete, and that members of the colonial services no longer have anything to learn from its study. I think the situation is not so simple. In the first place, here is the most striking possible example of uneven change. A small number of educated persons are about to operate the political machinery of a modern state with an electorate consisting mainly of illiterate peasants, to whom the implications of an electoral system are entirely new, and the problems of central administration largely meaningless. I admit, of course, that all modern government is the activity of a minority of individuals aware of the issues among a more or less indifferent mass. But I would maintain that, in those countries of western civilisation where the voter is allowed to exercise a choice, the gulf in experience and in values is not as wide as it is in the colonial and ex-colonial territories. And I would add that, in any case, studies of the type that anthropologists make, on the attitudes of the general public towards political issues, could be very informative in the so-called civilised countries.

In sociological terms the problem for the colonial peoples is a problem of re-integration. For today's generation the village and the tribe no longer enclose the world. The appeal of the market draws men outside. The opportunity of gain is followed rather than the path of duty, or rather, duty is forgotten when it hampers the pursuit of gain. We constantly hear of Africans who cannot advance themselves because if they are better off they are supposed to keep their poorer kinsmen, and these latter are invariably described as hangers-on or parasites. But there must be at least as many cases of old people past work who are neglected because the solidarity of the extended family is breaking down. We have not seen the development of any alternative to the obligations of kinship as a source of assistance to the needy, and we are not likely to as long as the small wealthy classes maintain their present aversion to taxation. Without going outside the bounds of African society, the organisation of production is beginning to depend on wage-labour instead of family co-operation—excellent as long as there is some recognised standard regarding the respective obligations of employers and employed. But is there? In parts of Nigeria sons demand payment for working on their father's farms. The father's right to command had gone by the board. What will take its place?

Anthropology cannot give the answer to these questions. But it can claim a certain merit for having asked them. Apart from anthropologists, few persons associated with colonial territories, indigenous or immigrant, even know that they exist, though many are aware of anxieties or dissatisfactions the causes of which they have not analysed. The anthropologist is the expert with the requisite knowledge for making such an analysis.

Some anthropologists have claimed that they could not only find the causes of the dissatisfaction but remedy them. But the remedies they have offered have either been remedies which were already advocated on grounds of common sense or common humanity—such as securing to indigenous peoples land sufficient for their subsistence —or else they have consisted in urging that nothing should be done to make the maladjustment greater by destroying indigenous institutions. This is another reason why anthropologists are called reactionaries. As I have said, we see now that that answer is no answer. We cannot solve the problem of uneven change by trying to prevent change. We must seek to stimulate the necessary further changes that follow from the initial ones. The problem is, as Mr. Furnivall has put it, how to make people want what they need.

Nobody at present has a very satisfactory answer to this problem. Colonial powers have tackled it at the material level by external pressure of various kinds. They all have their policies of village improvement in which they seek to induce the peasant to build better houses, to keep his village clean, to preserve the fertility of the soil, and so forth. They are all perturbed to find that persuasion works too slowly and compulsion leaves no lasting effect after it has been withdrawn. In England a year or two ago a conference of administrative officers from Africa was held which discussed for ten days the question how to stimulate initiative among Africans.

Africans have their own answer—'Leave us to ourselves and give us an opportunity to use initiative; then you will find it there'. But this only brings us to the crucial problem of finding the type of initiative which will be directed to the general good and not solely to the advancement of the cleverer or more fortunate individual. Mr.

Furnivall sees the answer to all these questions in the force of nationalism. He thinks that if nationalism is not just treated as subversive activity, but allowed to operate as a constructive force, it will inspire the indigenous peoples to the efforts which are needed to construct a new society. He points to the example of the rapid increase in literacy in Russia and China when those two countries decided that it was time for them to catch up to the level of the west.

It does seem clear that nationalism can give a very great impetus to the adaptation of indigenous institutions, and a much stronger one than can ever be given by a foreign ruler. But I cannot help wondering if the nationalist leaders themselves are not still impatient with the peasant's proverbial apathy and conservatism, and wondering how to overcome it. An anthropologist here would ask whether the problem is not the outcome of a conflict of values. The peasant farmer of the tropics is not lazy, as anyone who has watched him at work can testify. But in a subsistence economy, he cannot profitably do more than a certain amount of work, and so he learns to value leisure. When he awakens to the attractions of a cash income he does not cease to value leisure, and this makes it impossible for him to compete with those who value cash to the exclusion of leisure. Laziness is a relative term, with different meanings in different cultures. That is the anthropologist's analysis. It does not point to a course of action, but it does show, in one very simple example, why the habitual course, of upbraiding the peasant for laziness and preaching the virtues of hard work, is not effective. It suggests that it would be fruitful to investigate further the problem of incentives, to ask when and why does the peasant work hard as it is, what are his wants and ideals, to which of them can you appeal if you consider it necessary, in his own or the general interest, that he should work harder?

In general terms, I think I would say that the difference between the anthropologist's attitude towards these questions and the layman's is this. The layman supposes that for a colonial peasant community to develop into a modern state the separate individuals must develop the qualities that we think appropriate, and that we think we have— diligence, honesty, punctuality and so forth. The anthropologist's analysis shows that what is needed is the development of institutions, of appropriate systems of co-operation to which the appropriate values will be attached. But it also shows that to create the forms of these institutions is not enough. We can create them, but we cannot inform them with the values that we consider appropriate to them. The aims of the people who operate these institutions cannot be dictated. Here we have to leave it to the indigenous peoples to work out their own solution.

I mentioned that we are about to introduce a constitution based on universal suffrage in the Gold Coast. In Nigeria, elected local government bodies, with full constitutional responsibility for public services within their areas, are to come into operation next year. There is much speculation about how efficient they are likely to be. Will they balance

75

their budgets? Will they take bribes, or insist on the employment of their own relatives, or steal from the funds? The anthropologist will ask rather different questions. He will look at them in their wider social context. What social classes are represented in them? Who are the people who make their will effective, and why? Do certain persons carry weight in virtue of their wealth, their family connections, or other relationships outside the council? Is there in fact any link between them and the people who will pay the taxes that they spend? Above all, are they going to be a means of associating the peasants with the management of their own affairs, or of consolidating an indigenous governing class?

I would not claim that, in relation to any aspect of colonial society, the anthropologist can do more than improve the analysis of developments by widening the range of the questions that are asked.

But there is one respect in which he can pronounce with certainty to the effect that existing policies, if they are continued, will make the emergence of a re-integrated society impossible. I would suggest that there are two pre-requisites for a satisfactory adaptation, and that in a considerable number of colonial territories these are absent. One is that those persons who have acquired modern skills and adopted modern values should be able to take their place as full members in the new commercial society, and the other is that the new economy should not involve the separation of men from their wives and children. As I said, in many places these conditions are not fulfilled. To take the second first, the reason is that agricultural production for the world market has rarely been based on the enterprise of individual peasants. Perhaps this would have been impossible in some cases. As a matter of historical fact, there are many where it was never tried. Estate production involves the concentration of a large labour force at a small number of points. Mines demand armies of thousands, and hundreds of thousands. The necessary population is never present at the outset in the near neighbourhood. If the situation had been met by the migration and re-settlement of whole populations, the social problem of developing for these new communities common standards which would be appropriate to an entirely new type of life would have been hard enough. In practice this solution was in any case impossible. If the new enterprises had had to wait for the spontaneous migration that built up the large industrial centres of the western world, they would never have become established at all. Indeed, they could not establish themselves without recourse to measures of force or fraud which the world today condemns, or at least without condoning such measures. This action was justified by the argument that in primitive society the whole burden of production is borne by the women, so that to make the men work for wages is to confer a benefit upon the whole community. The question of the ethics of compulsion in this form is no longer a live issue. Today the impersonal force of circumstances sends Africans on their journeys of hundreds of miles to the Rand gold mines or the Copper Belt, and we are now beginning to discuss the ethics of compulsory restriction on this movement. But many people still assume—or policy is framed as if they did—that the African men—and the South Sea Islander and the coolie in Oceania too—is a detachable part of the society to which he belongs, and can be removed or returned to his place according as European enterprise does or does not need him. This assumption is convenient for people who hold it, because it absolves them from many responsibilities that either the employer or the State must bear in a modern community—to provide family houses, pay a family wage, social services, insurance against those risks which either did not arise in the old subsistence society or were met by an appeal to the duties of kinsmen. If these things are not provided, it is impossible to build up an integrated society with the wage-labour of the able-bodied men as its economic basis.

But the pre-existing tribal societies are already in a state of dis-integration, and the prime case of this is the migration of the men to the centres of employment.

It is not only anthropologists who have noted this; as soon as any considerable proportion of the men begin to go away to work the results are apparent almost to the casual observer; on the economic side in houses falling down, ground not cleared for planting and consequent shortage of food, on the social, in deserted wives and children growing up without paternal control. Government agencies in most African colonies have counted the number of men away and know their proportion to the total manpower, and the figures them-selves are regarded with alarm; in certain areas, anthropologists have examined the facts more closely and traced out in detail the effects on the societies concerned. Their studies reveal the profound internal contradictions of a society in which wage-labour is indispensable and which yet is not allowed to be a society of wage-labourers—a society whose accepted necessities include some which can only be bought for cash and others which can only be produced by direct labour, so that though work abroad is necessary, its product is not a substitute for work not done at home.

The most striking fact that these inquiries have shown is that under this system the economic requirements of the 'labour reservoir' societies cannot be met by the available man-power, since to meet them the same man would have to work simultaneously in places hundreds of miles apart. The younger men, working for their father's tax, their marriage payment, the equipment of a house, clothes for their children, now have the role which in Europe we call the bread-winner's—but bread is the one thing which they do not procure, and in their absence their families are short of food. Examination shows that the periods of absence of the wage-earners from their homes are growing longer and longer, their visits home not only more infrequent but of shorter duration. There is not, as might once have been hoped and is still in some quarters assumed, a rhythm of alternate work in the town and on the farm; there are long absences at work with short holidays at home. At the best, the absentees send money and goods home to their dependants; at the worse, they forget them and form new ties in the towns. In either case, the village in the tribal area is a place of women, children and old men.

The population of the towns is equally unable to become a coherent society. It consists predominantly of young men, either unmarried or with wives whom they have left at home. They do not stay long in one place, but travel to and from the rural areas and move from one town to another as they change employment. It is no longer assumed that they form the entire urban population. Most of the large cities now make some provision for family housing and also allocate land where Africans can build their own houses. A few mining companies provide quarters for their own employees. I think that on the Katanga mines there is a house for every African who actually has a wife. This is not the case in any British territory, and in relation to anything that has actually been found possible it seems a Utopian ideal.

Where living room is provided, it is hardly ever enough for a family with adolescent children or adult dependants. In these circumstances men hesitate to bring their wives to town and parents do not want to see their daughters go. Parents in the towns, if they have a sense of responsibility for their children, send them away to relatives in the country as soon as they are past infancy. It is almost impossible for old men past work to live in the towns, yet old people in the tribal areas may have no one to support them because all the members of the younger generation from whom they could claim it are away at work. Thus the traditional society of the native areas is being broken down, but there is no new community growing up outside. But if any social values are to be stabilised and preserved, they must be handed down from one generation to the next, and this is not possible if the generations are not in contact. In this system only a small minority of the younger generation maintain such contact with the elder. Again, for public opinion to be an effective social force there must be a group of adults in continuous contact; this condition is not present in the great majority of the urban populations. I say nothing of the poverty which forces Africans in the towns to means of livelihood that are contrary to the law. From the administrative point of view this is the major problem, and it adds disastrously to the difficulty of building up a coherent society with no standards. But the root of the difficulty is the constant change, the lack of continuity, which is regarded with indifference where it is not deliberately engineered.

These are not esoteric mysteries. The facts are widely known and many people besides anthropologists are concerned about them. But I have tried to present them so as to show how the anthropologist interprets them from his point of view as a specialist.

We have to ask too whether he can be no more than an interpreter. I think the answer depends on two questions—whether he is able to recommend courses of action, and also whether the public in general believe that he is.

On the first point he is in the same difficulty as other social scientists. He is dealing with the sum total of the actions of whole populations, and that can only be controlled to a very limited extent. We sometimes think the 'practical man' makes the mistake of thinking that colonial populations are infinitely malleable, and warn him not to imagine that he can mould them exactly as he pleases. But if we imagine that, because we know these populations, we can claim to decide what policy ought to be, we are making just the same false assumption about our own compatriots. Popular prejudices and vested interests will not disappear at a word from us. Moreover, it is very rarely possible to offer a specific solution for a particular problem. The situations in which the problems arise are too complex. A pessimistic social scientist once went so far as to say that all that any social science can tell you is how not to make things worse. Certainly many of our researches have done more to reveal unsuspected difficulties than to make it easier for governments to attain their ends. We can often trace the disintegration of a peasant society, but we cannot prescribe the cure. We can only say what I have tried to say— that the prospects of recovery are more favourable in some places than they are in others. If we were to urge that the destructive forces should be restrained, that we should deliberately keep the traditional institutions in being for the sake of social integration, we should be silenced by the voices of the colonial peoples themselves. Among them the older generations regrets the good old days, but the rest demand full membership of the modern world. Besides, change has gone too far for that remedy. The only way to remove the present maladjustments is by further adaptation.

The second condition is the attitude of the public towards us. Special knowledge cannot carry weight unless the lay public recognise its existence and wish to use it. Experts are called on to advise on malaria control because it is accepted that malaria is an evil and that the experts can deal with it; or on building roads and bridges because we are agreed on what we want in roads and bridges and we know who can give it us. But social integration is a commodity the general public have never heard of, though they may be aware of some of the consequences of social disintegration, such as the prevalence of crime. Yet this is the only subject on which we can claim to speak as experts. We may criticise colonial policies on general ethical grounds. Many of us do, and other people use the data we have collected to support this kind of criticism. But we are not experts on social justice. We are just unusually well informed laymen in that field. We have no right to claim that our view of social justice should be accepted *because* we are anthropologists.

What then is our contribution to the ends of colonial policy? Those in authority are apt to value information only so far as it helps them to attain ends they have already chosen. If they are told that their aims are unattainable, or contradictory, they dismiss such conclusions as 'impractical', and also the studies that lead to them. This consideration

79

limits the field in which Governments expressly ask the help of anthropologists. So we might have expected that at the present time, when the whole weight of Government support in Britain is given to the encouragement of westernisation, our studies would be officially regarded as obsolete.

Fortunately this is not so. On the contrary, since the Colonial Development and Welfare Fund was created in 1940, the financial provision for research in anthropology in the British territories is better than ever before, and we do not have to depend on the generosity of American foundations, which used to be our principal source of support. Some of the investigations that this fund has made possible have been dictated by the personal interests of the workers, but others have been carried out at the request of governments who believe that they can utilise the results. Most of the major regions of the British colonial empire have been surveyed from the point of view of their needs in sociological research.

The type of work that is being done under these auspices concentrates on the process of change and its results. One field in which these consequences call for practical action is that of customary law—those systems of enforceable rights and obligations which all governments, however much they may have made rapid Europeanisation their aim, have found themselves forced to recognise to a very large extent, since they reflect the relationships of daily life which are not changed by a stroke of the pen. Records of customary law may be obtained in various ways—by the comments of assessors on cases brought before European judges, for example, or by questioning selected informants. The special contribution of modern anthropological technique to this study is that it observes how the rules operate in practice, with all the evasions and compromises that are not mentioned when they are formulated in response to questions. Though there has seldom been much response to provisions intended to enable individual Africans to place themselves under the provisions of European law, abandoning that of their own custom, we are finding today that custom does not provide rules for all the situations that arise, notably in relation to commercial dealings. The gaps and uncertainties in the law administered by native tribunals today have engaged the attention of lawyers and could profitably be studied by anthropologists also.

In the special field of land tenure a number of studies are being made by anthropologists at the request of governments. The holding of land in a subsistence economy is so intimately bound up with the organisation of groups for economic co-operation and so with the general social structure, that this is emphatically a subject on which the anthropologist's approach is important.

The type of work he would do in this connection may perhaps be taken as an example of the contribution which anthropologists believe they can make towards the understanding of colonial problems. They do not seek to recommend action so much as to lay a finger on maladjustments, to indicate trends, and to check the accuracy of current assumptions. In this case, how is the system of land rights changing in response to pressure on the land, to the introduction of ploughing, to commercial cultivation, to changes introduced perhaps as a result of other influences in the accepted principles of inheritance? Does it still give security to the cultivator in occupation? Is every man still able to claim somewhere the right to land for subsistence? Does this claim conflict with the aims of commercially-minded farmers who seek to establish unrestricted control over the land they have cultivated with cash crops? Is it a fact that a few individuals have secured large areas of land in a manner which renders others landless?

Another example of a recent study carried out by official request was an investigation of the social position of women in the British Cameroons, made with a view to finding out how education for girls could be best introduced. Anthropologists have taken part in nutrition surveys, in the studies of labour migration that I have mentioned, in some places they have compiled handbooks of native law. A number of social surveys have also been made which cover such points as changing family structure and marriage law, family budgets showing how the balance is changing between subsistence and cash economy, the structure and composition of newly-formed urban populations, emergence of new types of association, and so forth.

Not many of these studies produce proposals for specific action, and I would suggest that it is really a mistake to judge the ultimate value of the anthropologist's work by this criterion. In the long run, he can take his stand securely on the contention that every addition to our knowledge of the processes at work in colonial societies must be valuable. Its benefit is more likely to be felt as the indirect result of its gradual diffusion among persons having administrative responsibility, increasing their understanding of the situations with which they are dealing, than in direct recommendations on policy. In the conflict of values which is the central feature of colonial societies today, the anthropologist cannot claim to be the arbiter. The question, for example, whether a particular departure from customary behaviour is enterprise or exploitation is not capable of objective determination; it is determined in fact by a complex of competing interests and competing values, and no longer, in modern days, by paternal governments who can at least profess Olympian impartiality. It is better then that the anthropologist should be content to put his knowledge at the disposal of the framers of policy, leaving to them the responsibility for decisions into which other considerations must enter. He can fairly claim that governments would be unwise to disregard altogether the facts that he lays before them, and dismiss as 'reactionary' all those aspects of indigenous custom and social structure which present obstacles to the attainment of the ends they have chosen. Facts cannot be annihilated by ignoring them, and in the complexity of social change in the modern colonial world there is more, not less, need to know what they are than in the past.

LONDON SCHOOL OF ECONOMICS
MONOGRAPHS ON SOCIAL ANTRHOPOLOGY

Titles marked with an asterisk are now out of print.

*1, 2. Raymond Firth, *The Work of the Gods in Tikopia*, 2 vols, 1940.
*3. E. R. Leach, *Social and Economic Organization of the Rowanduz Kurds*, 1940.
*4. E. E. Evans-Pritchard, *The Political System of the Anuak of the Anglo-Egyptian Sudan*, 1940.
 5. Daryll Forde, *Marriage and the Family among the Yakö in South-Eastern Nigeria*, 1941.
*6. M. M. Green, *Land Tenure of an Ibo Village in South-Eastern Nigeria*, 1941.
*7. Rosemary Firth, *Housekeeping among Malay Peasants*, 1943.
*8. A. M. Ammar, *A Demographic Study of an Egyptian Province (Sharquiya)* 1943.
*9. I. Schapera, *Tribal Legislation among the Tswana of the Bechuanaland Protectorate*, 1943.
*10. W. H. Beckett, *Akokoaso : A Survey of a Gold Coast Village*, 1944.
 11. I. Schapera, *The Ethnic Composition of Tswana Tribes*, 1952.
*12. Ju-K'ang T'ien, *The Chinese of Sarawak : A Study of Social Structure*, 1953.
 13. Gutorm Gjessing, *Changing Lapps*, 1954.
 14. Alan J. A. Elliott, *Chinese Spirit-Medium Cults in Singapore*, 1955.
 15. Raymond Firth, *Two Studies of Kinship in London*, 1956.
 16. Lucy Mair, *Studies in Applied Anthropology*, 1957.
 17. J. M. Gullick, *Indigenous Political Systems of Western Malaya*, 1958.
 18. Maurice Freedman, *Lineage Organization in Southeastern China*, 1958.
 19. Fredrik Barth, *Political Leadership among Swat Pathans*, 1959.
 20. L. H. Palmier, *Social Status and Power in Java*, 1960.
 21. Judith Djamour, *Malay Kinship and Marriage in Singapore*, 1959.
 22. E. R. Leach, *Rethinking Anthropology*. In preparation.
 23. S.M. Salim, *Marsh Dwellers of the Euphrates Delta*. In preparation.
 24. S. van der Sprenkel, *Legal Institutions in Manchu China*. In preparation.